D1102709

COMPASSION
& COMMUNITY

COMPASSION & COMMUNITY

Ordinary People with an

Extraordinary Dream

Illtyd Barrie Thomas

Copyright © 2005 by Illtyd Barrie Thomas

This edition copyright © 2005 by Piquant Editions Ltd
PO Box 83, Carlisle, CA3 9GR, UK
Website: www.piquant.net
E-mail: info@piquant.net

ISBN 1-903689-32-5

All rights reserved.
No part of this publication may be reproduced, stored in a retrieval system, or
transmitted in any form or by any means—for example, electronic or mechanical,
including photocopying or recording—without the prior written permission of
the publisher. The only exception is brief quotations in printed reviews.

A catalogue record of this book is available in the UK from the British Library.

Unless otherwise stated, Scripture quotations are from the *Holy Bible, New
International Version*, copyright © 1973, 1978, 1984 by the International Bible
Society. Used by permission of Hodder and Stoughton Ltd. All Rights Reserved.
'NIV' is a registered trademark of the International Bible Society. UK trademark
number 1448799.

Cover design and photographs by Diane Bainbridge
Book design by 2aT, www.2at.com
Printed in Great Britain

Contents

List of Photos vi

Foreword by Bishop Graham Dow vii

Preface ix

1 A Minor Miracle with a Major Message 1

2 The Vision 4

3 Business & Calling 11

4 Loaves and Fishes 15

5 An Unexpected Turn 20

6 Finding a Base 24

7 Our First Youthworker 27

8 Leaving the Old 29

9 Raffles Youth 31

10 The Bird 34

11 Wheels 37

12 Moving On... 43

13 The Grove 49

14 And On... 53

15 A Place for Everyone 56

16 First Fruit 58

17 Operating Principles 61

18 Back to School 64

19 A Worshipping Community 69

Afterword 77

Appendix 1: Stories that Illustrate some Practical Lessons Learned 79

Appendix 2: A Biblical and Theological Basis 95

Contact Info 102

List of Photos

Photo Insert A

- Early days: a Songs of Praise Christmas celebration
- The once disused Salvation Army hall is now the home of the Raffles Community Church.
- Sarah (and a friend), Kath and Jane on a Living Well outing
- The Family Centre
- Having fun learning practical parenting skills...
- ...or mastering some crafts
- In August 2003, BBC1's Garden SOS got stuck in round the back of the Centre...
- ...and this is the result!
- A place to sit and socialize
- Loaves and Fishes provides food for the stomach and the imagination.
- Two lads on an excursion with Graham and Zak

Photo Insert B

- Some of our volunteers show off their awards.
- Helping people to live well: the Trust brings health workers to Raffles...
- ...and gives young families the chance to relax off the estate.
- Older girls can hang out at The Grove...
- ...while after-school clubs offer dance & drama and storytelling.
- Open for business: the Den at Morton School*
- The right kind of problem
- Our first 'graduate', Rebecca*
- On The Bus: three of our youthworkers, David, Judith and Graham...*
- ...and some of our many satisfied customers

Copyright by Cumbrian Newspapers Ltd. Used with permission

Foreword by
Bishop Graham Dow

This book is a little gem. It's easy to read and it tells a remarkable story, of what God has been doing on a Carlisle estate called Raffles. My calling as Bishop of Carlisle has led me to pray for the city I have lived close to for over four years and I have seen some of this story as it has developed. My knowledge of some of the people involved, along with this account of their work, has given me a huge admiration for those who heard God's call and responded.

This is, above all, a story of God doing things, in his way and his time. For the four Christian people at the heart of it, it's a tale of persevering, unconditional love and acceptance for the people of Raffles. It has meant hearing God's clear word to them to share with that community not only the gospel but, first and foremost, themselves. It has meant investing their whole lives and beings in the community and slowly earning its members' trust, a trust noticeably foreign to the lives of so many people as a result of their low self-esteem and poor circumstances. This is incarnational mission after the pattern of Jesus, as the second appendix explains.

The story begins with a vision which unfolds slowly. There are periods when little seems to be happening, but this is important time for preparation and learning. This is a book about learning to do things God's way and waiting for his perfect time.

The story is full of the practical wisdom that is the fruit of this journey, wisdom that will benefit every serious disciple who seeks to work for Christ. So we learn that it isn't the needs of the people that the team seeks to meet but rather the people themselves, with their needs. In turn, the people of Raffles discover that they have skills that are needed in God's mission of compassion on the estate. Much misbehaviour has to be faced, for example in the children's club Loaves and Fishes, but these dedicated Christians grow to understand it. Often it's a way young people try to avoid going home to distressing circumstances.

At the beginning and for several years thereafter, the work was with children and women, brought by bus to the original mother church away from the estate. In the last four years, however, God has provided both a Family Centre and a Community Church on Raffles itself. The Bus, a doubledecker equipped to serve young people, now visits several parts of the city. Children excluded from school are successfully given a new start and an education. People's lives are being changed, and some of their stories appear in an appendix. To tackle all these projects, the number of both paid and voluntary workers has grown rapidly in recent years.

This is not only a lovely read, it's a story that makes me say: 'Lord, you are wonderful!'

Note: The Rt Revd Graham Dow is the Anglican Bishop of Carlisle.

Preface

This is the story of how the Living Well Trust and the Raffles Community Church came into being, bringing a holistic message of hope and healing to the local community on what had become a depressed council estate in the north-west of England.

The story starts more than 20 years ago with the vision received by one member of a small church nearby. From there things didn't develop in a structured way, according to a strategy that was carefully planned in advance. Rather, each stage of development happened in dynamic response to what God was busy doing. In a very particular way, it has been the result of 'putting one's hand in the hand of Jesus' and then stepping out to 'walk by the Spirit'.

At the heart of the work is the team of workers. Each one will be quick to say they are 'just an ordinary person', but if you met us it would soon become clear that each of us has exactly the temperament, the gifts and the life experience necessary for the task they are doing. As the work has grown, the vision and values have stayed the same but the strategies adopted to fulfil that vision have had to change. It has meant that we've had to grow and change along with the work. New people have joined the team, but the one thing we all have in common is that we want to bring the good news of Jesus Christ as Lord and Saviour to everyone who has not yet heard it in a way that makes sense to them in the full reality of their daily lives!

The main part of this book tells the story through the eyes of the people who were involved in the earliest stages of the work. It is not the full story, since that continues, but it is the story so far... Appendix 1 summarizes some of the practical lessons we have learned through the stories of the people of Raffles whose lives have been impacted by the gospel. Appendix 2 is a more technical summary of the biblical basis of the work as a 'compassionate ministry' of the Church of the Nazarene.

At the heart of our story are three important words that inform the work on Raffles today: loved, accepted and needed. For that is what we are, in Christ—and so that is what we embody to the people we meet. To the extent that a person knows and experiences the reality of these three words in their own life, their relationships will be transformed!

Barrie Thomas
Carlisle, 2005

1

A Minor Miracle with a Major Message

Sunday, January 11, 2004 is a wet and rather miserable day on Raffles Estate in Carlisle. From early in the morning there has been an excited bustle at the former Salvation Army hall. The building had been bought by the local council some 10 years before to be developed for community use, but it had since fallen into disuse. Recently the council has made it available to the Living Well Trust, which runs a family centre just across the road, and the Trust has refurbished it. Local people have said that they need their own church on the estate, where they can feel at home, and so today the hall is to be officially dedicated as the meeting place of the new Raffles Community Church!

After the opening of the Living Well Trust's Family Centre in 2001, it became feasible to have a weekly service there on a Sunday morning. Although only a few people turned up on any particular Sunday, a large number attended in total. People on the estate do not find it easy to commit themselves to a weekly event, but tend to come and go as their circumstances allow.

From this little group, the Raffles Community Church was constituted. Barrie Thomas, the director of the Trust and an ordained minister in the Church of the Nazarene, became its first minister. Now, as he thought about the forthcoming official opening service of the church in its own venue, just across the way from the Living Well Family Centre on Shady Grove Road, he had a strong conviction that on this occasion he should not do the expected thing and invite a large number of people from all the supporting churches and organizations in Carlisle. Instead, it should be a special day, set apart for the people of Raffles.

* * * * *

Two weeks before the opening I had had a strong sense that God wanted to show himself to this group of young believers in a way they would understand. So in the service that Sunday morning I had challenged them. I asked them to go home and pray that God would show them how many chairs we had to put out on the special day. They had to ask God to give them the faith that that number of visitors from the estate would attend the opening.

If every single person came who had been attending the church over the last few months, there would be around 70 or 80—but in a typical week attendance could be as low as 25. People from the estate are reluctant to commit themselves to anything on a regular basis—for them, life is too unpredictable.

The next week in church, I said: 'Last Sunday, I asked you to go and pray about how many chairs we should put out for the opening. Now I want you to close your eyes and then tell me what God has shown you by raising your hands when I get to the number he told you. Shall we put out 50?' I asked. No hands were raised. 'What about 75?' Still no hands. 'A hundred?' got three hands, '150?' a few more. But at 200 all the remaining hands—and by far the majority—shot into the air.

To put out 200 chairs would mean filling the hall. It would also mean having to borrow extra chairs for the occasion. But not even for a moment did I question the number they had chosen. Two hundred it would be.

The next Sunday, there was a sense of excitement at church. People were arriving in groups and carrying in dishes of food, as we usually served a meal after the service. This Sunday was to be a special celebration, a family feast. There was a great atmosphere of eager anticipation.

By the time I had welcomed everyone and begun the meeting with prayer, there was only a handful of empty chairs. By the time we sang the last of the opening worship songs, the church was packed, with not a spare seat to be seen. Two hundred people had turned up, and most were from the estate!

God indeed answered the prayers of his people on Raffles, and they celebrated and worshipped him in return. Their faith felt invincible. God was their champion. As far as they were concerned, he had performed a miracle, just to tell them that he was there!

2

The Vision

The story of how Raffles had declined to become one of those acutely depressed and underdeveloped council estates that are to be found on the fringes of cities all across the UK is by no means unique.

Built at the end of the 1920s as part of a regeneration plan for the city of Carlisle, at a time when slums were being cleared throughout the country, Raffles was thoughtfully designed around a central park. Its tree-lined avenues attracted residents who took a real pride in their new homes. The houses were not luxurious by today's standards but they did represent a significant step up the social ladder for their owners. Gardens and allotments were lovingly cared for, and as lately as the mid 1970s there was a waiting list of up to eight years for houses in this area. It is difficult to reconcile that fact with the present condition of the estate. In its prime, it had some 1,500 houses, but almost half of these have since been demolished in the last few years due to lack of demand.

Humanly speaking, there are many explanations of why things degenerated so badly. Some people blame bad decisions by the local council, which relocated feuding families to Raffles and housed them close to each other. Others look to bigger social changes, such as the cycles of unemployment that followed the closure of different labour providers in and around Carlisle. Some point to the development of supermarkets around the edge of town, which undermined small local producers.

Whatever the reason, the workers of the Living Well Trust today do not believe that the negative spirit that entered and spread over the estate was the result of poor management, failing economics or bad politics alone. They identify something darker behind the general depression, which they believe is a spirit that must be worked and prayed against in the name of the Lord Jesus Christ. The bondage of fear that has trapped many of the residents in a destructive lifestyle that is passed from one generation to the next can be broken only by the good news of Jesus Christ. And the Church of Christ has been called to put that good news into practice so that it is not just pie-in-the-sky by-and-by.

It was easy for those living on the estate to feel that everyone had given up on Raffles, including God. But all along there have been individuals who continued to trust that he had a special plan for both them and the people of Raffles. One person testified that she had received a very clear personal message of comfort more than 40 years ago from Isaiah's words in chapter 54:

> '*O afflicted city, lashed by storms and not comforted,*
>> *I will build you with stones of turquoise,*
>> *your foundations with sapphires.*
> *I will make your battlements of rubies,*
>> *your gates of sparkling jewels,*
>> *and all your walls of precious stones.*
> *All your sons will be taught by the Lord,*
>> *and great will be your children's peace.'*

From 1948 to 1968, the Church of the Nazarene on the neighbouring more prosperous Belle Vue Estate ran a Sunday school in the Raffles community hall, which was about a mile and a half away from the church. Many of today's older residents went to it, and even those who didn't can remember it well. It was characteristic of the smallish Nazarene denomination at the time to focus on evangelism, 'compassionate ministry' and education, but that emphasis faded during the 1960s for various reasons. As a result, the Belle Vue Church decided to close its outreach work on Raffles in order to concentrate more on its own, immediate community.

But in the 1970s a new generation of believers emerged at the Belle Vue Church who had a particular passion for Raffles. One of them, herself a resident of Raffles, was a young mum called Kath Queen. She was hardly the most obvious candidate to become a 'missionary' to the increasingly beleaguered estate, but she was very concerned about the growing atmosphere of suspicion and distrust and had a vague but strong sense that God could make a difference.

Kath had grown up in a nominally Catholic home and from an early age had been taught to pray before going to sleep at night. One person who made a huge impression on her was the woman who was later to become her mother-in-law. 'I met her when I was only 15,' she recalls. 'She always talked about Jesus as if she knew him personally.'

One Sunday in 1968 Kath decided to go to her mother-in-law's church, the Belle Vue Church of the Nazarene. 'Mostly it was because I could no longer resist her—she was always urging us to go to church.' That night the minister preached on Isaiah 1:18: 'Though your sins are like scarlet, they shall be as white as snow; though they are red as crimson, they shall be like wool.' Kath was moved by these words and, when the opportunity was given, she went to the front and someone prayed for her; but she was disappointed because she felt no immediate change. In addition, she had several traumatic experiences in quick succession after this and it was several years before she managed to get back to the church again.

Although she wasn't a Christian then, she remembers that in 1975 she prayed before she went for an interview at the local primary school for a job as a teaching assistant. She had little understanding of what she was promising at the time, but she vowed that if she got the job she would 'honour God' with it.

By the time Kath did go back to the church, in 1978, there was a new minister, the Rev Wesley Hands. She was very impressed with the way he handled her father-in-law's funeral. Shortly after, the five-year-old daughter of one of her relatives died very suddenly and Kath was shocked when she realized at the funeral that, had it been her, she would have had no assurance that she was headed for heaven. Still, when a Dick Saunders evangelistic crusade was held in Carlisle a little later, she refused to go. No, thank you! She had been disappointed once already and she didn't want to repeat the experience.

Meanwhile, at home things were tense. Then, one Saturday, after a terrible row with her family, Kath went upstairs to pray. As it was Whitsunday the next day, she decided to go to church, but when she got to the Church of the Nazarene she realized that it was a communion service. She wondered whether to take part, since she wasn't at all sure that she really was a Christian. In the end she did stay and took communion—and immediately a deep sense of God's peace flooded over her. When the congregation sang 'What a wonderful change in my life has been wrought since Jesus came into my heart,' Kath knew that he had indeed come into her heart, and this time to stay.

As a teaching assistant at the school, Kath got to know most of the families on the estate. Her own circumstances were far from happy. It was a struggle to make ends meet and she could well empathize with other struggling mums. She soon became known locally as someone who really cared.

Then, one Sunday in late 1989, Al Jessop from the Gospel Missionary Union visited the Belle Vue Church to preach on the theme 'Are you planting a new field for harvest?' He challenged the church to get into action and, more specifically, to identify what new 'field' they were called to cultivate for the gospel. Kath felt the challenge very personally: 'As I heard the preacher, the words went right into my heart. God spoke to me.'

That night as she prayed, God gave her a vision: 'I can't remember all the details, but there were three parts to it and people were being saved. There were families involved, and health work, but I'm not quite sure what the third part was.' It reminded her of the strong sense she had had while listening to Al Jessop's message earlier, that God wanted the church to get actively involved with the people of Raffles. And she had a very clear idea that the way to start would be to open some kind of drop-in centre on the estate.

Kath felt as if she was on fire, but for most of the church's members that particular Sunday passed like every other. She started patiently sharing with a few close friends what God had shown her, confident that it was just a matter of time before the whole church caught the vision, but no one seemed in a hurry to get very excited. In fact, church life continued as usual.

Kath knew that what she had felt and heard was not just something hare-brained she had made up. In the months that followed, God confirmed it to her again and again, through a Bible verse here and a remark in a sermon there. One verse that kept popping up was Jeremiah 1:5: 'Before I formed you in the womb I knew you, before you were born I set you apart; I appointed you as a prophet to the nations.'

It gave her a deep sense of assurance. Though she often felt lonely and in many ways life was difficult, it reminded her that God was committed to her in an intimate and unfailing way: 'As I saw other folk on Raffles struggling, I longed for them also to be able to have that assurance of God's love.'

A year later, in 1990, Kath heard the Rev Gordon Thomas, a lecturer from the Nazarene Theological College, speak on Isaiah 49:

> *Before I was born the Lord called me...*
> *He made my mouth like a sharpened sword...*
> *he made me into a polished arrow*
> *and concealed me in his quiver.*

For Kath it felt as if these words of God had been spoken directly to her. She understood that he was preparing her to be a useful tool for his glory on the estate.

As conditions on the estate degenerated physically, socially and morally at the beginning of the 1990s, the lives of those who lived there were increasingly under threat. Children suffered especially and Raffles was no longer a safe place to bring up a family. Riots were taking place, smaller in scale but every bit as serious as those in Toxteth. Whether they were a response to the poor conditions or an expression of anger by disaffected young people, or were simply mindless violence, the result was that the estate soon slumped even further and became a byword for crime and disorder, a reputation it has retained to this day.

And then in 1991, at precisely the darkest time in the history of the estate, God spoke very clearly to Kath again, and this time he said, 'Now! Now is the time for you to get to work on Raffles.'

Kath was completely confused. Surely this was not a good time to start an evangelistic outreach ministry on the estate! She didn't doubt that she had heard God's word correctly, but she needed others to confirm it. So, she asked God for a sign—like Gideon, she put out a fleece. 'Yes, God,' she prayed, 'but if this is really what you want me to do, tell someone else! Tell Barrie!'

To this day, she can't say why she prayed that prayer. Barrie Thomas was a member of her church and he served alongside her on its board of management, but they were not close friends and they were not involved in any joint ministry. He was one of the directors of a haulage business with an annual turnover of £100 million; Kath was a teaching assistant at the local primary school. People at church tended to give Barrie a wide berth. He seemed to be the archetypal successful big businessman.

But, having prayed that unusual prayer, Kath didn't waste any time. At the first available opportunity, a Saturday-evening Scrabble social at church, she took Barrie aside and, getting straight to the point, asked him urgently, 'Has God been speaking to you, Barrie?' He gave her a strange look. The question obviously came like a bolt out of the blue, and he couldn't truthfully say anything but 'No.' But that didn't bother Kath. She immediately and confidently replied: 'He will.'

Barrie was dumbfounded. Something extraordinary was afoot. Was this God's answer to the prayer that had been quietly stirring in his own heart for some time?

3

Business & Calling

Barrie had grown up in a small town just outside Carlisle. His parents both became Christians when he was four years old, and after that the family worshipped at various independent churches in rural communities around Carlisle.

* * * * *

I gave my life to Jesus at the age of eight and I was mentored by a very gifted and inspiring local Brethren teacher and lay preacher, Reg Maiden. When I left school, I went to work for an accountancy firm but quickly knew that this was not my life's calling—though I did learn solid financial skills there that have served me well over the years. I went into industry as an accountant but when the engineering company I worked for ran into financial trouble during the oil crisis in the 1960s I suddenly found myself unemployed.

I soon found work with the British Deaf Association as a project manager, but the experience of unemployment made a deep impression on me. Only a month earlier I would have looked down with scorn on the unemployed people I now worked with in the association's video production unit. I used to believe that unemployed people were either lacking in skill or plain lazy. I was amazed to discover the huge amount of untapped talent there was in these people, and the sad circumstances that often led to their being unemployed. I also learned sign language and became aware of the harsh realities of life for many people suffering disabilities.

I met my wife Jane at the local YMCA. We both enjoyed the buzz of working with people. After we got married, we bought a house on the Belle Vue estate in Carlisle and decided to join the local Church of the Nazarene. Neither of us came from a Nazarene background, but we felt comfortable in the Wesleyan tradition in which the church stands. We wanted to be part of a local worshipping community and there was a new young minister at the church, the Rev Wesley Hands, and a general atmosphere of enthusiasm. In the Methodist Church, I had been a Boys' Brigade leader and I hoped to use that experience at Belle Vue. Jane and I were aware of the nearby troubled Raffles estate, but we never went there and for all practical purposes it didn't exist, though we knew there had been a small outreach work from the Belle Vue Church long ago.

In 1986, I left the British Deaf Association and joined a small local haulage company. I was ambitious and worked hard, and the company expanded very quickly. But however hard I worked, I always continued to be involved in the church or the community as a volunteer.

For a while I served as the secretary of the local Christians in Sport group, and it was in that capacity, at an event in the Midlands, that I was introduced to a young man from Carlisle called Graham Slater, who had just given his Christian testimony in public for the first time. We immediately developed a good rapport, never guessing that our paths were to cross again!

At church I was invited to join the board of management. Kath was also on the board, but we didn't really know each other as friends—most members of the church kept their distance from me in those days. I was quite a closed, private person and I guess, looking back, I must have appeared aloof to most of them. At the time it didn't bother me too much, as I always felt I was more of a 'backroom boy', the one who got things done behind the scenes. I usually opted for the role of treasurer—I didn't see myself as one to lead from the front.

Then, when I was 32, my father died.

My dad had been the natural leader in our family. Somehow it seemed proper for him to take the spiritual lead at family get-togethers, and other members of the family would come to him for advice when they had to take difficult decisions. I didn't really appreciate this until he was no longer there, when suddenly it was as if his mantle had fallen on me. My relatives now turned to me for spiritual advice. It was a frightening experience, for which I didn't feel ready at all.

I realized I needed God's help and it was a time of deep spiritual awakening for me. At one communion service God spoke to me powerfully and I wept as I prayed for forgiveness and knew I had to commit myself to him. I felt his love washing over me in waves. It was as if he was saying: 'I want more of you. You are too comfortable where you are.' I gladly made myself available and even went to talk to our pastor, but he couldn't give me any clear guidance on just what the next step should be. So I offered myself for full-time Christian work, assuming that opportunities would soon open up, but nothing happened. Jane and I both stood up at the Keswick Convention mission meeting in 1990, and I even applied for jobs with some mission organizations, without any success.

The thought crossed my mind that I might go into the ministry but as I had no theological training at the time it was quickly ruled out as quite impractical. In the end I decided simply to work harder in the church. Every time Jane and I made ourselves available for full-time Christian work, God seemed to be saying, 'Well, thank you for your willingness, but the time is not quite right yet.' Moreover after each of these occasions I received either a substantial pay rise or some other success in business. It was as if God was testing me all the time to see whether I would still be ready to give it up for his sake.

I love physical sport and I play hard. I have always worked aggressively at being the best I can possibly be in whatever I am doing. It wasn't long before I was promoted to be the legal and commercial director of the Eddie Stobart Group, the once small local haulage business which by now had become a conglomerate. I guess that to many people

I seemed very fortunate to have realized what surely must have been my highest ambitions. But that job turned out to be only a stepping stone to what I now consider to be my life's work, though I didn't know it at the time.

When Kath challenged me on that Saturday evening in 1991, I immediately knew that God was speaking to me through her. Perhaps he didn't want me to be in full-time ministry but wanted me to support someone else. Perhaps I was the one to stand beside Kath and help her turn her vision for the people of Raffles into a working reality. I could start by helping her promote the idea and by encouraging others to get involved!

4

Loaves and Fishes

Once Barrie grasped God's call, he and Kath decided that the next step would be to get the formal blessing of the church on this initiative. They had an appointment with the pastor in the autumn of 1991. 'I've never seen a man go white as quickly as he did when Kath told him the vision God had given her,' Barrie remembers. The pastor, a godly man, realized that he wasn't called to this work himself, but he didn't hesitate to encourage Kath to get started and he undertook to pray regularly for her and for the work. Kath was very relieved and thankful to have his blessing and support.

Up to now Kath had been expecting that she would be an assistant or supporter to someone else who would lead the work. But now it was dawning on her that the call she so passionately believed in was not directed at the church but very specifically at her. She was to be the worker! Barrie was tied up with the Eddie Stobart Group and, although he was now also deeply committed to the needs of the people of Raffles, it was clear to them all that God had given the vision to Kath and that it was through her that he wanted the work to start.

In retrospect, too, Kath could see how 25 years as a teaching assistant in the local school had been God's perfect preparation for this moment. During that time she had learned to love the people of Raffles in a tangible way, as one of them, and she could understand how hard it was to live and raise a family on the estate. Through her work with the children, she had gained the trust and respect of the local families. And, though it seemed inconsequential at the time, it was that trust and respect, built up by her commitment and perseverance over many years, that formed the foundation for what today looks like the runaway success of the Living Well Trust's work on Raffles.

Kath still nursed the idea of a kind of drop-in centre on the estate. She decided to start with a regular coffee afternoon for women in what had become known as 'the Green Hut', a wooden building at the centre of the estate. She planned and advertised a simple programme of crafts with a relaxing drink and a snack, open to anyone who wanted to get out and meet their neighbours. Admission would be free, for Kath well understood that even a small fee could be a major deterrent to people who lived from hand to mouth. The plan seemed sound, appropriate, helpful—but it was a disaster. Not one single woman turned up. However, the place was overrun by children!

So, in the spring of 1992, Kath started a children's club on Raffles. It was called 'Loaves and Fishes'—appropriately, for these children are often really hungry. It would have been impossible to 'minister to their hearts' when they were tired and apathetic because there was no food in their stomachs, and so Kath was quick to recruit a small army of bakers from the ranks of her family and friends. She was still working as a teaching assistant in the week, and so at first the club was held fortnightly on a Saturday afternoon. By popular demand it soon became a weekly event. To this day, the Living Well Trust continues to run Loaves and Fishes as well as other after-school clubs.

From the very beginning, Kath was blessed with a faithful and fearless helper and friend, Fay McGowan. Together they faced the crowds of children, whose behaviour defied all rules and norms. What was involved in the meetings? Food, lots of singing (the children loved learning songs), storytelling and a lot of crafts—there is nothing Kath and Fay can't whip up out of a couple of empty toilet rolls, a few bits of coloured card, some string and a stick of glue!

Kath and Fay have mixed memories of those early days, but one image that remains particularly vivid is of their soft-spoken pastor standing out in the cold, patiently pleading with some youngsters to come down from the roof of the Green Hut before they should fall and hurt themselves! His gentle remonstrances were drowned out by the wild whoops and whistles from aloft.

Kath had a much more down-to-earth approach: one warning and then the threat of no food. She wouldn't plead with them, she would simply close the door. The realization that they were excluded, while they could hear the others having a good time inside, was a much more effective way to coax the rascals down. Once again the dear pastor was quick to acknowledge that he would probably be of more use praying for Kath and Fay than trying to lend them a hand!

Many lessons, still useful today, were learned in those early weeks. For example, it took a long time to understand that the children's 'bad' behaviour, especially towards the end of a session, arose not out of malice but simply from the fact that they dreaded going home and needed the extra attention for as long as they could get it! Many of these children have never experienced genuine personal love and care before.

Kath is the first to acknowledge that she and the team of volunteers who have joined her over the years have made many mistakes and had many embarrassed moments. But they tried never to make a mistake at the cost of any child. They knew that the most important thing of all is persevering, unconditional love! But there is a cost involved in giving that sort of love, and Kath often felt tired and burdened at home. She also started to suffer from backache.

Working with children is usually regarded as women's work in the church, gentle and unchallenging. But Loaves and Fishes was physically, emotionally and spiritually exhausting. Week after week, month after month, Kath and Fay and their volunteer helpers kept going. No one received any money for their labours, which were officially an 'outreach ministry' run under the auspices of the Belle Vue Church of the Nazarene.

'What was most difficult at that time', remembers Kath, 'was that we never had a place of our own and never knew where we'd be meeting next.' This was the situation after the Green Hut was deliberately burned down by some of the older youths from the estate. After that, groups had to meet in various other community buildings on the estate, even in a disused Portakabin in the school grounds. None of these venues were ideal. In addition, it became clear that other groups on the estate were doing their best to stop Loaves and Fishes getting regular access to certain buildings. Apparently, winning the trust of the children and being open about the Christian faith were a formula that antagonized other community workers. But Kath's team was not doing it in their own strength or for their own purposes! They were resolute and certainly wouldn't give up because of so 'trivial' a matter as a building. They faithfully kept going in this way for another eight years.

Other initiatives were tried in this period, such as women's keep-fit classes and other adult clubs; but all failed. No one could understand it at the time, but with hindsight it is clear that God had serious plans and was not going to skimp on the time he needed to train his helpers. Patience was one of the first things we had to master, and it's not a theoretical subject! It means learning to trust in God's provision alone and to accept that his timing is always perfect. Obedience, too, had to be learned in practice. It meant not getting tripped up by apparent failure but learning to 'lose face' graciously for God's sake and try again.

While other ventures failed, the children's work continued, attracting a regular 20 to 25 children each week (which, as it happened, was the most the available space could accommodate). Sadly, when the children reached the age of 11 there was no other club for them to move on to. Many who had attended Loaves and Fishes for several years were 'lost' at this stage, and Kath longed to see a youthworker specializing in meeting the needs of the teenagers on the estate.

Although she was learning to be patient, at times she felt very low and frustrated. It seemed as if the work was going nowhere, and yet she had been given a vision to realize and not for one moment could she lose sight of it. But in reality very important progress was being made. The people of Raffles were taking note. They already knew Kath from her work at the school but they had to assess her in this new community role. They were watching to see what hidden agenda was driving her.

Today, people from the Raffles estate know all about the Living Well Trust and perceive us as 'good people—people who always seem to do good'. One person summed it up like this: 'What people on Raffles have come to appreciate about the Trust and its workers over the years is that they are people who do what they say.' Therein lies the value of all the heartache and frustration Kath and Fay suffered—they were necessary to break down a huge barrier to trust and acceptance, and God was doing just that! What people see is love in action, not techniques.

'It's amazing,' says Kath. 'You think you are giving out love, but the love you receive in return is always so much greater. If God gives you the love, you have to give it out—you can't do anything else. And when you do that, he just keeps giving more!'

5

An Unexpected Turn

Although Barrie was still working at the Eddie Stobart Group, it made an enormous difference to Kath to have his strong support and constant interest. Then, in 1996, just as it seemed that things would never change, the time was suddenly right for the next step.

At a conference of Nazarene Compassionate Ministries, Gustavo Crocker spoke on the theme of 'fishing in deeper waters'. Inspired by the account of Jesus' instruction to his exhausted disciples recorded in Luke 5, he challenged his listeners to get out of their comfort zones, those places where they felt secure and in control, where they never really needed to rely on God. Both Kath and Barrie liked to be in control and for them this was a whole new way of thinking. And it was very scary.

Several things then happened in quick succession. Barrie was responsible for the financial and legal sides of the Stobart Group and as a result he was often away from home for long periods of time. In fact, he spent so much time in the Warrington/Manchester area of the UK that he decided to buy a house there instead of living constantly in hotels. He found a suitable property in Didsbury.

* * * * *

Often on these trips I would think about Raffles and wonder what more I could do to help Kath. I felt frustrated because nothing much seemed to be happening. With hindsight it is so clear to see that if any stage had been cut short, Kath and I would not have gained all the experience we needed and we wouldn't have been properly prepared for the task ahead. It's no coincidence that God kept me in business until the time was absolutely right for the Raffles work to move into its next exciting stage of development. Maybe, if God had shown me then a picture of what lay ahead, I would have been too frightened to continue!

Meanwhile, I discovered that Nazarene Theological College was literally round the corner from our new home in Didsbury and so I decided to enrol for part-time evening classes. I had by now had a clear call into the Church of the Nazarene ministry and I assumed that God wanted me to become a non-stipendiary, 'bi-vocational' minister, doing unpaid pastoral work alongside my work for the Stobart Group. I obtained my local minister's licence in 1996 and could officially start my clerical apprenticeship.

In April 1998, at another NCM conference, Gustavo Crocker's challenge was reaffirmed by Herman Gswandtner, who focused on the need to turn the world upside-down by becoming 'agents of change'. He defined an 'agent of change' as someone who was given over completely to living a compassionate lifestyle 24 hours a day, seven days a week, 52 weeks a year. By 'a compassionate lifestyle' he meant one that served 'whole' people, not just meeting their perceived spiritual needs but connecting with all the experiences of their daily lives. The fruit of the actions of agents of change in a community, he said, was summarized in Acts 13:41: 'Look, you scoffers, wonder and perish, for I am going to do something in your days that you would never believe, even if someone told you.' It is nothing short of social transformation!

Both Kath and I realized that we were meant to live as pilgrims, to become flexible and adaptable, not constrained by commitments to the things of this world. Only then would we be able to reach out with the love of Jesus (and not secret selfish ambitions) to cross barriers and make meaningful relationships with the people we were called to serve.

* * * * *

Meanwhile, there were job cuts at the school where Kath was working. She was now 50 and there was a chance she could apply for early retirement. But it wasn't her dream to retire early in order to enjoy off-peak package holidays! Her family depended on her salary and she still had a vision to realize on Raffles. If only she could find a way to continue to supplement her family's income, early retirement would release her into full-time work on the estate!

So she 'put out a fleece' for the second time. This time she prayed very specifically that if it was God's will that she should become a full-time worker on Raffles, he should confirm it by providing a particular sum of money in response to her application for early retirement. When the official papers came back, she found that she was offered exactly the pension package she had prayed for! In addition, a supporter raised the funds to pay her a salary for a further six years.

Then, one Sunday evening in the early summer of 1998, in the middle of a church service, Barrie felt a sudden and excruciatingly painful pressure across his chest.

* * * * *

It felt as if my chest would collapse, but I didn't want to cause Jane any anxiety, so I just excused myself by saying I was feeling unwell. The next day I was still in great pain and had to admit that it was more serious. I ended up in hospital, wired up to various machines and told to lie still until further notice.

To cut a long story short, after numerous tests it was determined that I had 'hit the brick wall'. The level of stress I had endured, and indeed come to thrive on, had caused a sudden physical collapse. I was told in no uncertain terms that if I continued at the pace I had been going, the next attack would be far more serious than this 'warning' one had been. I needed no convincing. I explained my situation to my fellow directors at the Stobart Group and it was decided that I could resign over the next six months (to allow a good transfer to the person who would follow me).

I had no doubt that this was God's way of making me move on. He knew I was available before, but it wasn't possible to leave a job like mine just like that. For one thing, the company had 2,500 employees and I couldn't just walk away from such a big responsibility. Many people have never understood how I could do it at all. As far as they are concerned, one doesn't surrender a powerful job or the sort of salary I had. But it wasn't that hard for me. God had made the decision an easy one.

At the same time, I took a determined next step: I decided to have the work on Raffles formally constituted as a charitable trust under a trust deed. In September 1998, I became the part-time, unpaid director of the new Living Well Trust (as I was still officially employed with the Stobart Group until the end of the year). I also invited leaders from several different church denominations and Christian organizations in Carlisle to sit on the board of reference, which brought the work on Raffles to the full attention of local believers.

Kath received the news of her successful application for early retirement just as the Living Well Trust was formally constituted, and she immediately became its first full-time member of staff. By December 1998 I was the full-time director of the Trust—still unpaid until January 2005, when I started drawing a salary.

6

Finding a Base

There was still no obvious remedy to the constant headache of having to find a suitable venue on the estate for Loaves and Fishes to meet. In the past, they had been invited to organize special family services at the Belle Vue Church and people from Raffles were encouraged to go there. Both Kath and Barrie continued to be members and leaders of that church, and so they assumed that Living Well's work would in effect be an extension of its programme. They approached the church leadership for permission to use its premises for the weekly Raffles activities, and it was a huge relief when they agreed. At last, a fixed venue for Loaves and Fishes! Soon Kath was organizing other events, like a luncheon club for women—though the distance from the estate to the church meant that she had to arrange transport, especially on dark winter days.

Kath's 'office', however, moved to the streets of Raffles. She started spending the time she was not involved with Loaves and Fishes or other clubs simply 'prayer walking' around the estate and visiting families. Occasionally people would invite her into their homes and she began to build a web of the kind of relationships Herman Gswandtner had talked about. There was no visible impact, but her gritty perseverance was forging invisible bonds of trust—and in this community trust is the rarest of commodities.

The work continued like this for two years, with Kath walking the streets, visiting people in their homes and hosting the clubs in the church. Two important lessons were learned during this time which have been firmly incorporated into the Trust's way of working. First, 'the need is not the call'. This is an important principle to understand for anyone involved in compassionate ministry. The need is never-ending and if we focus on the need and become consumed with a passion to meet it, we can end up trying so hard to 'rescue' someone that in effect they become our persecutor and we become their victim. Only God can meet the need. No individual today can save the world. Jesus died to do that.

The second lesson learned in these early days was that we were called to 'meet people in their need'. There is a critical difference between meeting a need and meeting people in their need. If I offer to meet someone's need, I stay in control and it is easy to imagine that I am superior to them. This in turn can create the impression that I am arrogant, that I know the answers while they do not, that my way is better than theirs. Sadly, this was often the attitude communicated by British missionaries in the past, and the results of that suggestion of arrogance still haunt us today.

On the other hand, meeting people in their need, and following their agenda, affirms and empowers them. It tells them that they are valuable in my sight, that I respect their way of life. I may personally find a room with no carpet on the floor and no paper on the wall quite intolerable, but to some people carpets and wallpaper may be quite irrelevant. It doesn't mean they are wrong, it just means that I shouldn't impose my values on them. When we meet people in their need, we can share their pain, be useful as a friend and gain their trust.

Kath and her helpers noticed something else, something that prompted 'bad' behaviour among the children on the estate. These children are so used to people letting them down, so used to losing whatever attention they receive almost as soon as they get it, even at home (where a parent may frequently change partners), that they deliberately set out to 'lose' the attention before they are deprived of it. It's less painful that way. It took a long time for these children to grasp the fact that Kath and her team had a level of stickability they hadn't experienced before. To find that these people cared so much and were so consistent about it was a shock to them.

And it continued to distress Kath and her team that although they were meeting the needs of some of the children on the estate through Loaves and Fishes, once they reached the age of 11 or 12 they simply 'dropped away'. There was just not the staff or the facilities to arrange a regular programme for another age-group. The older boys especially needed a very different sort of programme to what Loaves and Fishes could offer. Many of them had been nurtured almost since the day they learned to walk, and it seemed sad to lose them on the threshold of their critical teenage years. Kath and Barrie started to pray for a dedicated youthworker to join the team.

7

Our First Youthworker

God uses ordinary people. Mostly they are people who have had an encounter with him in which they have experienced for themselves that he loves them, accepts them and has a special job for them to do.

In the summer of 1995, Graham Slater and his wife, Ruth, bought a house on the Belle Vue estate. One small decision Ruth made then is still causing ripples to this day! She had two young children and, as she didn't have a car and at that time no public bus could take a double buggy, she accepted an invitation from her next-door neighbour to attend the mums-and-tots group at the Belle Vue Church. She soon became a regular and, as she has an outgoing personality, quickly made friends with the local mums and their children. With hindsight, it seems no coincidence that Barrie's wife, Jane, was in charge of that group.

At this time, unknown to Ruth, the church's youth groups were struggling and help was needed to keep them going. The people in charge could see the enormous need but they simply lacked enough manpower. When Jane, half joking, suggested to Ruth that she ask Graham if he could help them out one evening a week, it didn't seem such a strange suggestion. Her husband is muscular and well versed in the local lingo. He had been a streetwise teenager himself and would not find it hard to relate to these lads. In fact, after only a few sessions it became obvious that he was exceptionally gifted in working with difficult youngsters like the teenagers from Belle Vue the church was working with at the time.

Graham could empathize with these lads because he too had been a rebel at school, with plenty of aggression. From early on he had been part of the gang of 'bad' lads, and he well remembers the day his secondary school headteacher dismissed him with the words 'You will never achieve anything with your life.' Then, when he was 15, his best friend was electrocuted while messing about in a railway shunting yard. Graham had never thought of himself as vulnerable, but now for the first time he saw how destructive his friendship with these lads could be. He also realized that he needed to make a drastic change. But how could he get away from them?

There was only one thing to do: he could ask to be put back a year at school and in that way get a clean break. And that is exactly what he did. God seemed to be one step ahead of him, because when Graham walked into his first class the only available seat was right in front of the only Christians in the class: two boys and a girl called Ruth.

These three were quick to befriend him. Graham had grown up in a Christian family but he had given God a wide berth up to now— until after one particularly bad day, in desperation after failing again, he opened the Bible that had been lying on his bookshelf for years, right at the story of the prodigal son. He read it, and has been hooked ever since!

'Some of the lads from that original gang are dead today,' he muses sadly. 'Some are drug addicts who are living tortured and unfulfilled lives.' Although Graham left school with only a few qualifications, he settled into a stable job driving a fuel tanker for a local firm, became very involved in a local church and married Ruth. They soon had a family. He was hardly looking for new challenges when he was struck by a visiting preacher's urgent question: 'You only have one life. How are you investing it for God?' It made him feel uneasy, and the feeling would not go away.

It wasn't a total surprise, therefore, when Kath and Barrie suggested that he leave his job driving tankers to work full-time on the streets of the estate as a 'detached' youthworker of the Living Well Trust.

8

Leaving the Old

While Kath was strolling the streets, Barrie enrolled at Nazarene Theological College in Didsbury to study for an honours degree in theology as part of his ministerial training. This meant that he had to spend two or three days a week in Manchester. At the same time, Kath and Barrie were experiencing a steep learning curve in the work on Raffles.

* * * * *

While at college, I came across a Bible verse in my studies that cut me to the heart. No doubt I had read it many times in the past, but this time I read it as if for the first time. 'So deeply do we care for you', Paul wrote in 1 Thessalonians 2:8 (NRSV), 'that we are determined to share with you not only the gospel of God but also our own selves, because you have become very dear to us.' I knew it was important for me—and for everyone who would join the Living Well team—to understand that this is the model for our involvement with the people on Raffles.

Kath and I had earlier learned very specifically that we were to 'go outside our comfort zone' and 'fish in deeper waters'. We had been instructed to become 'agents of change' through living a compassionate lifestyle. Now God was saying to us that that was not yet enough. We had to invest our whole life and being into the community, we had to share ourselves completely with the people we had been called to serve. Until now we had not understood even a fraction of what God was calling us to. Preaching the word was not enough, we had to live it, in full view of the people, with our faith as relevant to a family on a wet Wednesday afternoon as it was to a single person in a Sunday service. We had to 'walk the talk', as they say.

When I shared the verse from 1 Thessalonians with Kath and Graham, it came as no surprise to them. It was as if God had already prepared them to receive the challenge. It was an immense confirmation that our business was not to make our own ideas happen—God was calling us, and he was equipping us for the next stage.

I received my district minister's licence in March 1999 and in October 2002 graduated in theology from the Nazarene Theological College, which is an affiliated college of Manchester University. In 2003 I was ordained as a minister in the Church of the Nazarene.

9

Raffles Youth

The young people growing up on Raffles Estate have a bad reputation in Carlisle. Many spend their days mainly on the streets because they are excluded from school and threatened or unwanted at home. They have little self-esteem and have no motivation to co-operate with the educational programmes that are provided for them. Others are the main carers in their families from as young as 10 or 11 years of age. Some are on medication for behavioural problems. Although they often appear confident and aggressive, most are desperate for attention—desperate to find love, acceptance and meaning for their lives.

It was a big step of faith for Graham to accept the job the Trust offered him, and the drop in salary it involved. But he and Ruth had prayed about it and it was their joint decision that he should make this career change. So, in January 2000 Graham became the third full-time member of staff of the Living Well Trust. Ruth immediately started doing part-time secretarial work for the Trust to supplement their family income.

As a detached youthworker, Graham would not be operating from a fixed venue but would be walking the streets of the estate, much as Kath had done previously, to get to know the young people in their daily environment, gain their trust and become part of their scene. Although he seems the ideal youthworker and has a natural rapport with young people, his first year turned out to be the most difficult of his whole working life.

By spending long hours out and about on the estate, Graham was soon at home with the local dialect, in which 'Mangnix, the

31

muskir racking' means 'Say nothing, the police are here' and 'That's cowie' can mean anything from 'That's brilliant' to 'That's disgusting' (and the locals always know which). Still, despite his hard work, there seemed to be something preventing him from winning the young people's trust. He often felt very low when his attempts to befriend them met only an abusive response. It was almost a full year before he got to the root of the problem.

Being suspicious by nature—part of a strategy to safeguard themselves against getting hurt and being disappointed—the youngsters had spread a rumour that Graham was an undercover policeman! Once he realized this, all he had to do was to call on some old acquaintances from his own rebellious youth, many of whom were now parents of the young people he was trying to reach. With their co-operation, the word started to spread and things began to change.

Youthwork provides many heartaches but also many amusing or memorable moments. One of the first Living Well family outings was to an outdoor centre near Carlisle. When the time came to get back on the bus for the journey home, one strapping 12-year-old lad simply wouldn't budge. All attempts to get him into the bus failed. Today the Trust workers would not be surprised by such behaviour, because they have come to understand that when these children realize that a happy session is coming to an end, because they don't know what they are going to find when they get home—or maybe they know only too well!—they just want to stretch out the time as long as they possibly can. Many of them have become conditioned to think that there is only one way for them to keep the good times going and hang on to every last bit of attention: namely, to be as difficult as possible! On this particular occasion, there was no alternative but to do a fireman's lift and hoist the lad onto the bus.

Another very typical incident occurred on a family trip to a children's farm in the Lake District. One young boy, on medication for attention deficit hyperactivity disorder, was carefully assigned an adult who had to supervise him the whole day. But somehow, with amazing speed and agility, he managed to escape over the barrier into an enclosure where a huge sow was suckling her litter and boldly went to sit on her back! Imagine the horror of the rest of the group, who tried to coax Joe back while making as little commotion as possible so as not to upset the sow! When he was finally retrieved, his supervisor asked him with a sigh of relief and exasperation: 'What shall we do with you, Joe?' The little lad smiled contentedly and, without a moment's thought, replied: 'Just give me my tablet and I'll be all right.'

10

The Bird

A Harris' hawk is not exactly the sort of co-worker one expects to find in the youth ministry of a Christian charity. Eagles maybe, doves certainly, but a hawk...? Yet just such a bird provided an important breakthrough in gaining the trust of the Raffles community. This is how it happened.

Graham was targeting the older teenagers and as a result he also made contact with many of the unemployed young men on the estate. Their lives were usually an unbelievably complicated tangle of hardships outside their control mixed with the results of immature or foolish behaviour. By being available to them and having the time to talk to them where they were, Graham started getting their attention. But a big step forward in one relationship would often result in some sort of repercussions elsewhere. People were hurting. Many had suffered disappointment on disappointment. It wasn't easy for them to trust another new face and another new initiative.

Graham is a great animal lover and in the course of that tough first year he became aware of the important place hunting has in the world of the lads and men on the estate. The ultimate for them is being out at night in the fields with only a flashlight, a dog and a gun. But Graham is not a hunter and has no love of guns, and he realized that if he wanted to enter into the life of the community this area was something he would have to negotiate. However, he has always loved birds of prey and this gave him an idea.

So, the Trust funded Graham to be trained as a falconer and, as soon as he qualified, bought him his first Harris' hawk, a male called Zak. The bird fascinated the young people on the estate, and flying him gave Graham an opportunity to develop friendships with some very difficult 'customers'. In particular, it created an unthreatening context for one-to-one conversation.

One year when Zak was moulting and couldn't be taken out, the owner of the nearby bird-of-prey centre where Graham had trained offered him another bird to fly. It turned out that this larger female, Storm, was temperamentally better suited to the Raffles work than Zak. Meanwhile, one of Graham's contacts on the estate had become so keen on Zak that he offered to buy him. A deal was struck and the bird changed hands—but the next morning, to everyone's consternation (for such news travels fast on the estate), he disappeared!

The new owner immediately phoned Graham and they set off into the surrounding woods where Zak used to fly. And bingo! they spotted the bird high up in a tree. But Zak felt smug that day, and well fed, and they were unable to lure him to the ground. They decided to wait a few days before trying again, in the hope that he would get hungry, but by then Zak had vanished without trace. Again and again Graham went to all his favourite haunts, but there was no sight of the bird. After two weeks the situation became critical. Graham didn't need to be reminded by the owner of the bird-of-prey centre that unless the bird could be found in the next 24 hours there was little chance that he would survive in the wild. Zak now became the subject of fervent prayer by the Living Well team and their friends and supporters. It seemed as if the whole estate was watching.

The very next afternoon, as Graham turned into Shady Grove Road on his way to the Family Centre, he saw a small crowd of people gathered on the pavement staring up into the sky. And there, just three houses away from where his new owner lived, was Zak, nonchalantly perched on a rooftop. Graham screeched to a standstill and pulled out his mobile, and soon his friend from the bird-of-prey centre arrived with a lure, glove and blindfold. Moments later, Zak swooped down onto the glove. A sigh of relief rippled through the assembly—and the whole estate buzzed with the exciting news that God had indeed done a miracle on Raffles. Zak was back!

11

Wheels

While Kath and her team were running activities in the Belle Vue Church, it became one of Graham's tasks to ferry mums, toddlers and young children to and fro between Raffles and Belle Vue in a small minibus. Often he had to fit in several trips in both directions for a single meeting. But the older teenagers he was working amongst as a detached youthworker were more territorial and they were not very enthusiastic about meeting off the estate. It became clear that if the youthwork on Raffles was to progress it needed a dedicated meeting-place, and one on the estate.

It wasn't easy to find a suitable venue. Little help was forthcoming from the local council, whose initial offer of six small houses to be converted into a community centre was quickly withdrawn when they were scheduled for demolition along with 400 others on the estate. It seemed as if we had reached an impasse. By this time the Trust had grown and the work had branched out. Several community projects were up and running. One such venture was a furniture and clothes recycling scheme. Quite by chance one day as Barrie and Graham were visiting the place where the furniture was stored, they spotted a small bus that belonged to the King's Church in Keswick. Neither of them had ever considered such a conversion before, but the relevance to Raffles was immediately clear. A mobile youth centre! What a perfect solution!

No time was wasted, especially after Barrie had given Graham the challenge: 'If you can find the bus, I'll find the money.' And they soon did find one, a small 17-seater. But Graham had bigger dreams and, with a bit more pressure to 'find one quickly or we'll have to get that one,' he managed to locate a 35-seater, complete with on-board kitchen. Four-and-a-half thousand pounds made available by another Christian trust was spent in blind faith, but there has been no looking back.

Graham's practical experience as a tanker driver was put to excellent use in fitting the bus out. He also unashamedly sought sponsors. The city council was first to be approached, and its first response was to earmark electricity points in some derelict houses where the bus could be plugged in. System Driver Training generously provided free training for Graham to get his PSV driving licence. More recently, the Hadfield Trust has provided an on-board generator so that the bus can be entirely independent of external power points. It's a great advantage to be able to drive away from a potentially dangerous situation—or to move out of earshot when the music gets turned up full blast! Local companies were very generous in spray-painting the bus and donating and fitting electrical equipment.

The bus was a single-decker which Graham kitted out with a seating area, a small kitchen and a tuck shop. It boasted a sound system, TV and video, and offered computer games and board games like Jenga and Uno, sports equipment for outside games and literature on drug and alcohol abuse. What better name for all this than 'Operation 3:16'?—which at the same time served as an excellent conversation-starter! Up to 30 young people could fit on the bus at any one time, but over 120 different individuals are known to have used it.

In October 2004, just as this first bus reached the end of its useful life, the Trust received the gift of a double-decker from Stagecoach. Graham again kitted the vehicle out, but this time there was funding available to get much of the work done professionally. The new bus—which is now known simply as 'The Bus'—has two quiet areas and a kitchen, eight computer games consoles, a sound system and a 42-inch plasma-screen TV.

In its first month on the road, The Bus was visited by more than 250 'hard to reach' young people, and after six months the total had

Early days: a Songs of Praise Christmas celebration

The once disused Salvation Army hall is now the home of the Raffles Community Church.

Sarah (and a friend), Kath and Jane on a Living Well outing

The Family
Centre

Having fun
learning
practical
parenting
skills…

…or
mastering
some
crafts

In August 2003, BBC1's *Garden SOS* got stuck in round the back of the Centre...

...and this is the result!

A place to sit and socialize

Loaves and Fishes provides food for the stomach and the imagination.

Two lads on an excursion with Graham and Zak

reached 600! Such is the interest, not only from the young people but also from the council, that a second bus is being considered. As The Bus can accommodate up to 40 young people, more volunteers are now needed to support the team of full-time, paid youthworkers, which today numbers four. In this way the Trust has developed valuable relationships with the local YWAM discipleship training scheme as well as Operation Mobilisation and members of local churches in the areas where The Bus operates. We certainly couldn't operate without a lot of committed support!

'I have had a wide range of customers,' says Graham. Some stay the whole time the bus is open; others come just for 10 minutes—'but even that can be a breakthrough with kids who don't engage with anyone.' One key to the success of the two buses is Graham's clear conditions of entry. 'From the beginning, I've had only two rules: No one is allowed on when they are under the influence of drugs or alcohol, and everyone must show respect, for others, for the bus and for the equipment.'

It hasn't been easy to stick to these rules. The first one especially has been severely tested. But Graham is adamant that he will not be intimidated. He has had some scary moments though. One guy managed to get on board after taking an excessive amount of tablets. Half an hour later the drugs took effect and Graham had to muster all his strength and skill to get him off. Another person tried getting under the bus to set it alight. Someone has threatened Graham with a snooker ball in a sock, someone else has pulled an air pistol on him— and Graham has even driven off blissfully unaware that some young people had sneaked up onto the roof. Fortunately on that occasion a CCTV camera alerted the police and they stopped the bus.

But standing his ground has paid off. One of Graham's happiest moments came when for the umpteenth time one week he bumped into a gang of guys who had been giving him a particularly hard time.

'Is the bus out tonight?' they asked. 'And can we come?' He was on the point of replying, as so many times before, 'Yes, and you have to come straight-headed!' when they went on: 'We're going to come straight-headed tonight because we're sick of not being allowed on'! No wonder the council is taking notice and has asked if the bus ministry can be extended elsewhere—especially after the local police had started to report that whenever The Bus is out, the incidence of youth crime and anti-social behaviour drops significantly in that part of the city.

Graham is also committed to visiting those who have been banned from the bus the night before for misbehaviour. The very next morning he will be on their doorstep or will meet them out in the street. 'Let's talk about last night...' may open up some deep hurts. 'They're always embarrassed,' he says, 'and it's important to let them know that they're forgiven and are welcome to come back.' Is it hard to do this work? 'It is lonely,' he says, 'and I'm vulnerable.' Whoever does this work needs protection. 'Never being on your own with a young person is common sense and also good practice according to the Trust's child-protection policy. But prayer is the most important safety measure.'

Graham has never had a planned programme of activities for the bus. 'The kids come,' he explains, 'and they organize what they want to do.' Some Christians have been horrified to learn that he doesn't even insist on an epilogue! But Graham and his helpers answer every question seriously and they regularly create opportunities for questions of a spiritual nature. This is in fact the most rewarding part of their work, responding to questions about life the youngsters may never before have had the freedom to discuss with anyone older than them. Sometimes Graham is asked why he switched off a particular song, or what 'Operation 3:16' means. 'It's fantastic to share my faith with young people who come and ask questions. But until they do ask them there's no point giving them the answers!'

Not every employee of the Trust lives on Raffles. Is it important to do so? 'Not really', says Graham. He doesn't live on the estate and is very proud that he's been called 'an honorary Raffleite'. Some of the young people jokingly call him 'Dad'. 'To be trusted by them is a tremendous joy. I feel very privileged to share their lives', he says. He and his colleagues often receive tokens of appreciation, such as this poem by one youngster:

> In this world
> I'm walking upon,
> There are three people I
> can trust:
> Graham, Judith and God.
> They all let me express
> my feelings,
> although I still feel pain.

So, at the end of the day, does the integrity of a person's life speak louder than their words? Graham hesitates before answering this question. 'Well, it's a combination. How we live can speak volumes, but we have to speak up as well.'

There are sad experiences too. Without a doubt, seeing young people on drugs is among the saddest. 'Many folk can't understand why they do it,' says Graham, 'but when you hear what they've been through, and what they are not receiving, you understand. How would you live, for example, if your earliest memory was of abuse in the home, with no safe place or person to turn to? What would be your understanding of love then? What if you received no care, if you didn't know whether your parents would be sober when you got home, or if they'd be there at all? What if there was no food on the table and you were so hungry you couldn't concentrate at school? What if you felt you had ruined all your chances, and life held nothing worth dreaming about for you?'

Graham can speak from experience. When you ask him what has been the best training for his job, he doesn't talk about the diploma in youthwork he's doing, or the courses on drug, alcohol and gambling counselling he has completed. Instead he says without hesitation, 'My life before I became a Christian!' And that includes the prayers of his Christian parents. In God's economy, nothing is wasted.

12

Moving On...

There was one further lesson the team had to assimilate as part of our preparation for becoming God's good news messengers on Raffles. It has since become a guiding principle and a cornerstone of good practice for the Trust. It seems so obvious and so simple, and yet it is so profound.

In September 1999 Dr Don Wellman, the pastor of the First Denver Church of the Nazarene in the United States, was the speaker at a local Nazarene weekend conference. The theme for the weekend was 'Loved, Accepted and Needed'. The messages were based on Dr Wellman's analysis of the most important tools for church growth. With these, he claimed, you will be able to open up the hardest of hearts for the gospel of Jesus Christ.

He went on to explain that one of the most basic needs of all people is to be loved. But many have never experienced love in their lives, or have a distorted view that love always has a price tag: Do this or that and then I'll love you. The message of the gospel is radically different: that Jesus loves you no matter what and there's nothing you can do to make him love you more and nothing you can do to make him love you less. His love is unconditional and knows no bounds. And that is the love that we as his representatives are to show other people. We must reflect the unconditional love of Jesus we have come to know in our own lives, and we must pass it on to everyone we meet.

Because this love is unconditional, it accepts everyone. There should be no exception to this love. So many people have experienced rejection in their lives because of the way they look, the way they dress, their social status, their educational ability. Their standards may be different from ours, their priorities in life may be different, but Dr Wellman urged his audience to accept everyone as they are and not on the condition that first they must become what we want them to be.

For most regular churchgoers this is difficult. Can you honestly say you feel comfortable sitting next to a prostitute, a drug addict or a drug dealer? Wouldn't you rather sit in the same pew as the mayor? Unconditional love means unconditional acceptance.

In too many churches we still take the approach that people must first behave, then believe and then belong—whereas in truth we should be opening our doors to welcome people with our love and acceptance so that they feel they want to belong, and then they can believe and then they will behave. We shouldn't hit people with rule books concerning dress code and lifestyle priorities. Rather, we should hit them only with the love of Jesus, as evidenced in our own lives by the way we love and accept them as they are.

In John 8, a woman caught in adultery is brought to Jesus for judgement. He doesn't condemn her or give her a talking-to, but simply releases her into a renewed life with the liberating words 'Go, and sin no more!' This is far more powerful than a stern lecture would have been.

Not only are we to love and accept people, but we are to show them that they are needed. It is through being needed that people experience self-worth and develop self-esteem. On many occasions in their lives they may have been rejected or told that they didn't have the requisite skills, but within the church we are to find a suitable ministry for every individual. The Nazarene theologian W T Purkiser once wrote that within every church there is for every member a function to fulfil, and for every function there is a member who can fulfil it. The question is: Are we keeping our eyes open for the people who will fulfil all those functions? How do we know we can trust them to do them right? Or do we think (also as Christians!) that we are so special that, unless we can produce clones of ourselves to get the job done, we can't possibly share the work out?

By loving, accepting and needing the members of the community you are called to serve, you will discover the amazing truth that not only are you able to break down the barriers and get close to them but they in turn will show you that you too are loved, accepted and needed by them. That is one of the most humbling experiences, and a most deeply spiritual one too!

Kath and Barrie had been members and leaders of the Belle Vue Church for more than 20 years. The Raffles women's luncheon club was using the church kitchen and function room during the week, Loaves and Fishes had moved permanently to the church premises, the new Raffles boys' club was meeting there and a Bible study group from the estate had also started to convene in the church. The weekly programme of the Belle Vue Church had become dominated by activities related to the work on Raffles. It started to dawn on Kath and Barrie that this was not as promising a situation as it might at first have seemed: The church's regular members and its board of management didn't share their vision for the work on Raffles. Increasingly Kath and Barrie realized that it had been wrong of them to assume that sooner or later everyone would catch their vision. And in fact, although the people from Raffles attended services at Belle Vue and used the church building during the week, they never really felt at home there.

* * * * *

The sort of outreach ministry envisaged by Belle Vue for Raffles was simply so radically different from our growing understanding of our calling to 'be church' on Raffles that the two approaches could not be combined. As we had come to see it, we were called not to implement a social programme but to be the programme that brought the community together in worship.

As Kath and I became more absorbed in the growing ministry on Raffles, we also realized that we could no longer be effective members of the board of management of Belle Vue. Our focus of interest had shifted, and as soon as a new minister was appointed at the church the time was right for us to leave.

At the same time it was clear to the workers of the Living Well Trust that we had to find a suitable venue on the estate. We considered several possibilities, but nothing worked out. In the summer of 2000, after Graham had joined the Trust as its first youthworker, the city council approached us with the offer of two small houses we could convert into a centre. This we gladly accepted, though we realized that it wasn't the ideal solution—such a centre would be far too small for our dreams!

Then one day I was asked to lead the funeral of the stillborn baby of a woman on the estate who had become very special to us. Kath had been her birthing partner and was present when the baby died. Leading this service was one of the hardest things I have ever had to do, and Kath and I both felt weak, with little comfort to offer. But later that very day a letter arrived from the man who owned the local post office and convenience store. He had bought the former Co-op store on Shady Grove Road and was prepared to sell it to us for the price he had bought it for, provided we didn't open a shop in it! Kath and I knew that this was God's doing. It was as if he was saying to us: 'You may feel weak, but I'm strong. This is my gift to you.'

* * * * *

In November 2000, work started on converting the property into a family centre. By the end of that year the Trust employed three full-time workers and one part-time administrator, but it was also supported by many volunteers, of which a significant number came from Raffles Estate. Most of the latter are still working with Living Well today and are proud to talk about the training opportunities they've had and the skills they've developed that they never even thought they had. Marion Winder, Lesley Maddison, Maxine Mews, Ann Thomson, Denise Graham spring to mind immediately, people who truly care for their community and are prepared to put in hours of hard work week after week. Other volunteers who have come and stayed include Barrie's wife, Jane, who has helped out with the children's work for several years and then moved on to work with the over-fifties, and Val Underwood, originally from the Belle Vue Church, who has faithfully assisted with the children's work.

New paid staff have joined the team as and when the funds could be raised. Sarah Thomas, Barrie's daughter, was interviewed and employed—unknown to him!—as a youth and community worker developing parent-and-toddler programmes and pastoral care work. Penny Fearon joined the team as a youth and community worker after serving as a volunteer on Operation 3:16 for two years. Paul Cannon, who had twice been seconded by his college to work with the Trust, is now the full-time youth education manager, and David Smith, another long-time volunteer on the bus, recently left his job as a salesman to join Graham in detached youthwork. Piece by piece God is building his team on Raffles!

The Living Well Family Centre was officially opened in September 2001. It was custom-developed with a coffee shop, a meeting lounge and several offices and meeting spaces upstairs. One area was developed into a boxing gym, where Charlie Shepherd, the former world super-featherweight boxing champion, offered training classes (and an opportunity to get rid of pent-up energy!) for young and old. In addition, as it became clear that few local people had access to health provision because no GP or NHS services—particularly the services of a midwife—were available on the estate, the centre became host to regular clinics held by a midwife and a health visitor.

At the time, the Trust workers thought that the opening of the Family Centre was their ultimate achievement, the climax to many years of hard work. Little did they realize that it was only another step on a continuing journey that God was mapping out for them.

13

The Grove

When Graham joined the Trust full-time, Ruth was quick to offer her services as a volunteer. Barrie discovered that she was a dab hand at office administration, and Kath was just as appreciative of the puddings she contributed for the weekly women's luncheon club (her lemon ice cream is a particular favourite!). Ruth was easily at home among the women of the estate and they felt comfortable in her presence.

She had grown up as a missionary kid—her parents had been in Cyprus. During her early teens they moved back to the UK and she remembers well how she cringed when she walked into school the first day and realized that her unfashionable clothes and heavy shoes made her stick out like a sore thumb. She has never forgotten that feeling of being the odd one out and it made her sensitive to the fact that there were other children at school who were worse off. 'One girl came from a very notorious part of town and was always being heckled and called names. I remember feeling so bad for her.' These experiences have helped Ruth to identify with the young people on Raffles, who often have very low self-esteem. She also recalls that it was the young people's meeting at her local church that helped her to cope through those years.

So, did she always want to become a missionary herself? 'As an 11-year-old I accompanied my parents on a trip to visit the Operation Mobilisation teams working in Egypt. I saw people rummaging through mountains of rubbish to find food, and many were living in tombs. I can clearly remember this as the time when I became aware that I too wanted to be involved in mission work. I attended several youth missions in Europe as a teenager and assumed I would work overseas, but God has had a different plan for my life to date.'

At 16 years of age, she was doing a discipleship course at her church and they worked through a study in the Christian Disciplines volume of the Lifebuilder Bible Study series. Recently she was astonished to find her workbook and note that in answer to the question 'Describe some of the cultural barriers around you' she had written the following: 'Racial, eg in areas of Carlisle like Raffles etc.' She went on to say that what was needed were 'Christian day centres for the unemployed', not necessarily to concentrate on preaching but 'just places where you can befriend people and so share the gospel.' It is amazing to realize that Ruth was writing this just when Kath received confirmation from God that 'now was the time' for action to start a drop-in centre on Raffles!

At one staff meeting between Kath, Graham and Barrie it was decided that the Trust needed to develop a group for the girls who were approaching the upper age-limit of Loaves and Fishes. When Ruth typed out the minutes, she almost choked with shock when she read: 'Ruth to be approached to run a club for teenage girls'. The thought terrified her. 'I'm an administrator,' she thought. 'I can't do this sort of work!'

But Graham and Barrie were not easily put off and they encouraged her to give it a try. In the event, she took to it like a duck to water. She quickly developed deep friendships with the girls and they in turn found it easy both to like her and to trust her. It was obvious that God had given her a very special gift of compassion, as well as a practical and spontaneous temperament. Of everyone, Ruth herself was the most surprised to discover that she had such gifts and was so capable of doing this kind of work!

By this stage the refurbishment of the premises for the Family Centre was well advanced, and it became clear that the Trust would need more staff to meet the demands of the growing range of opportunities that were opening up to it. While Graham continued to expand the detached youthwork through Operation 3:16, Barrie and Kath noted that there was a parallel need for centre-based youthwork. It seemed that in particular what was wanted was a youth advisory service to offer guidance on education, employment, training and life skills to young people who wouldn't use the services available at schools or elsewhere in the city. Barrie managed to raise the funds for such a service and the Trust decided to advertise a vacancy for a part-time youth project manager.

As Ruth typed out the job description and personal profile for the position, she felt an intense longing to apply for it herself. She asked Barrie if she could and he said yes, but she would have to put in a formal application and undergo all the tests and interviews just like every other applicant.

Three candidates were selected for interview, and Ruth was one of them. They were all strong contenders with varied strengths and fields of expertise. On the day of the interview, Ruth felt very nervous. She desperately wanted the job but found it daunting to be questioned so closely by Barrie and Kath. The candidates were all given the same tasks and asked the same things, and she knew she would have to prove herself if she was to succeed.

Despite her misgivings, Ruth was appointed as the youth advisory service worker in July 2002. This new position needed a great deal of development work. For example, she discovered that there existed no one single local advocate for the needs of young people in the west of Carlisle, the area where Raffles is situated. So she started networking to establish a steering group of individual professionals working in education, health, the government initiative Connexions and the police, as well as those involved with existing voluntary groups working with young people. This group became a sounding board for her projects and they also co-operated with each other to ensure that real needs were being met and that services were not being duplicated.

Meanwhile, the group for girls who had 'graduated' from Loaves and Fishes continued under the new name of The Grove. Rather than just offering an informal time of fun, Ruth assembled a programme for the girls that looked at issues of self-esteem and taking care of their bodies and their environment. She drew on a range of existing resources for this but also developed some materials herself. 'I knew I could do admin and I enjoy being given a mess to sort out,' she reflects, 'but I never thought I'd be someone who young people could turn to, that I'd become a role model for them!'

At the same time she enrolled in a basic counselling training course and then started studying part-time for a degree in social studies with particular reference to children and family. The practical experience she has gained with the Trust, together with her ability to assimilate and apply academic knowledge, has now made her an expert in working with difficult young people and she is now asked to give seminars on the subject. This aspect of her work has also been a big surprise for Ruth, who is always ready to enthuse others with the vision and the love God has given her for the disadvantaged young people of Raffles.

14

And On...

In September 2003, in order to help Barrie with the growing load, Kath and Ruth became associate directors of the Trust. Ruth now has special responsibility for the youth education projects and Kath is the manager of the Family Centre and has special responsibility for family support issues. What a long way from those early days of Loaves and Fishes in the Green Hut! There are many volunteers now who help with the children's work, though it will always stay close to Kath's heart.

When she thinks back, she confesses that the work is harder now than in the early days. 'In those days we used the Belle Vue Church building for meetings and everything happened there—the women's luncheon club, the mums-and-tots get-togethers... The children were taken there by minibus. When it was over, it was done. But now the work is much more complicated. We work longer hours, and you never know what situation might present itself the next moment! One can't be prepared for everything.'

The Family Centre has become a hub of activity on the estate. Many happy memories involve trips, which are a regular feature of the work. On one occasion, around 150 people met at the centre to go on a daytrip to Scotland. 'It was a red-hot day,' Kath reminisces. 'But no bus turned up. We waited, but still no bus came. After some frantic phoning around, some buses were finally located and we left two hours late. The people were very patient, and everyone had a lovely day, despite the stressful start!'

Kath's own learning curve has not yet showed any signs of flattening out since she joined the Trust. She feels she has grown in the way she sees people—'They're not in boxes any more.' She has had the opportunity to do several counselling courses and other modules of study which have helped her to reflect on her own situation and work through some personal issues. What she teaches is not dry theory but a living, breathing reality in her own life.

Recently she had a very difficult year when she developed a bad back and 'became focused on pain.' She also suffered emotional pain, connected both with her family and with some particularly hurtful circumstances on the estate. How did she cope? 'By learning to lean more on God. I became so tired, I had to say "God, I'm sick of carrying two bags of coal. You said your burden is light."'

The Trust has expanded so fast, and so many complicated matters relating to finance, funding, planning, networking, strategy and the law now need attention. It would be easy for Kath to feel that she has served her purpose and there is no place left for her in this work. She confesses that 'when the youth education work started in the Trust, it seemed as if all the activity moved from downstairs, where I am based, to the upstairs offices. But we have talked about it, and my department too has now grown considerably.'

Above all, though, she knows she is not there by her own will but by God's appointment. She continues to be involved with Loaves and Fishes and in the counselling of parents of socially disadvantaged children, a new initiative that is a collaboration with local social services. Another area of concern to her is ministering to victims of domestic violence.

So, what has been Kath's personal highlight in her work with Living Well? 'We never impose talk about Jesus except in the Bible studies or church services, which people can choose to attend; but when people start asking questions about Jesus in other contexts, because they notice that something about the people here is different, that is a fantastic opportunity because they want an answer. And when people actually become Christians, well...'

Some of our volunteers show off their awards.

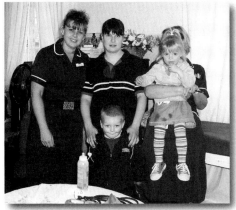

Helping people to live well: the Trust brings health workers to Raffles...

...and gives young families the chance to relax off the estate.

Older girls can hang out at The Grove…

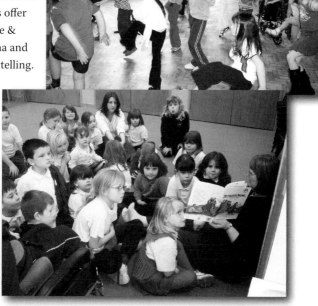

…while after-school clubs offer dance & drama and storytelling.

Open for business: the Den at Morton School

The right kind of problem

Our first 'graduate', Rebecca

On The Bus: three of our youth-workers, David, Judith and Graham…

…and some of our many satisfied customers

She loves to tell the story of one girl who joined the team for a short-term training placement. She was divorced and didn't find life as a single mum easy. She was also a newcomer to the area. 'She wasn't a Christian but she saw that we were different and after a while she started asking questions. Today her mother says: "I can't believe how she has changed." And she herself describes what has happened to her quite simply: "When I came to you, I was a biblical virgin. Now I'm a biblical babe!" And then she adds that with God in her life, she has been "given back the innocence of my youth but allowed to retain the wisdom of my years".

15

A place for everyone

There really is a very special place for every person in the work of
God. Some are given a vision, which encourages all who hear of it
with the knowledge that God is at work in the world today. Others
have leadership abilities or other strategic gifts and are able to give
structure to another person's vision, to put the necessary programmes
together. Some have practical skills or special skills in communicating
with particular groups of people. It's important to realize that no one
person is more crucial to the work than another. Moreover, what
many workers with the Trust have found is that their gifts are not
fixed. If only you're brave enough to step outside your comfort zone,
you may discover gifts you never knew you had!

One of the Trust's words of wisdom is that 'each member of staff
must find their replacement.' This is essential if the work is to continue
to grow and develop in the future. It also means that no one can
get absorbed in their own gifts, as everyone has to learn to actively
appreciate others and encourage them.

Of course, it would be disingenuous not to mention the hard
times. Often a breakthrough in some particularly difficult area will
be followed by a time of disappointment. Recently, for instance, after
the youthworkers had enjoyed a very positive week, some money
was stolen from the Family Centre. The only people there at the time
apart from the staff were a few old hands who they trusted. It cast
a shadow over some good relationships that had been built up over
many months, and emphasized our human weakness. On another
occasion a digital camera disappeared during a very happy time of

celebration—though in that case it was quietly put back a few days later.

But such reverses are forgotten in the joy at finding that even one young person who previously could not talk about their deep depression and lack of self-worth can now write a poem like this:

Thank you, God,

I found trust—and you.

It isn't easy for me to let

my faith in you be known.

A teen with the Lord in their heart,

—people make fun of them.

16

First Fruit

Judith Warnock is one of the young mums on Raffles Estate whose lives have been turned around through their contact with the Living Well Trust.

She became a regular volunteer for Loaves and Fishes and other after-school clubs and attended the Songs of Praise services with her family. She was always quick to offer help in any situation. One day she said to her mother, 'I don't know what it is that these people have, but I want it for myself.' Up until then she had been interested and had listened and looked, but she hadn't made any Christian commitment. This is a feature of outreach work in a needy community like Raffles—people find it very hard to 'commit' to anything. You can have a wonderful discussion and feel you have made great progress only to find that the other person then disappears for weeks or even months, and it can seem as if everything was in vain. However, that is rarely the case. It's just part of the emotional process that people who have been badly disappointed and are afraid to put their faith in anyone or anything else have to go through to establish trust.

Then, at 2am one morning, Ruth and Graham's phone rang. It was Judith, in tears, asking them to pray with her over the phone. She had decided she couldn't put it off any longer: she wanted to become a Christian there and then!

Judith is skilled in catering and when the Family Centre opened, she joined the team to run the café. She did that for about 18 months, but when she left we had a feeling that she would be back!

Once Operation 3:16 was in operation, Judith was one of the first volunteer helpers. She trained as a drug and addiction counsellor at the same time as Graham, so that they would be better prepared for the sort of problems they often faced on the bus.

In 2003 she returned to the Trust as an employee, working alongside Graham as a detached youthworker. She is now also heavily involved with the Trust's educational programmes working with children in danger of exclusion. 'It really is a miracle,' she says. 'I'm dyslexic. I didn't really go to school much after the age of 10. My mum was often badly treated by my dad, and especially after weekends I had to care for my younger brothers. So, I never really learned to read. But today I can use a computer and I make worksheets, write stories and dramas, take part in leading worship... I didn't do any courses, Ruth just showed me how to.'

For Judith, as for so many people who have grown up on Raffles, probably the greatest problem in life is low self-esteem. 'I used to try and destroy things when people said something positive to me. But now I've learned to take it and hold it as something lovely to be thankful for. Now when someone says to me, "Well done!" I imagine the biggest slice of thick chocolate cake you can think of, and then I imagine taking a bite and feeling it sliding down all the way into my stomach, and then I look at the person and say, "Thank you for saying that to me." It has changed my life!'

She goes on: 'I'm very happy when I can see a child learning this lesson. For example, one day a teacher complimented me on a display I'd put up at school, so I went through my routine and thanked him. He was so surprised to have someone respond in such an appreciative way that he remarked: "It's nice when someone appreciates a compliment—thank you!"

'So I told him about the chocolate cake. I noticed that there was a lad standing behind him who had heard it all and was giving me a very strange look.'

A few days later Judith was in school again and happened to be around when a teacher handed a piece of work back to that same boy. 'That was exceptionally neat and well done,' the teacher said. Normally the lad would have pulled his cap over his eyes and pretended not to care, 'but', she recounts, 'I could see him straightening his back. He raised his head and looked straight back into the teacher's eyes and said with a pleasant smile: "Thank you for saying that, sir!" Then he gave me a little sidelong glance. It was a brilliant moment.'

17

Operating Principles

When Barrie looks back at his time as a director of the Eddie Stobart Group, there is nothing in the practices or attitudes he adopted there that he feels he subsequently had to 'unlearn'. To the contrary, what he learned there has been crucial for the work on Raffles! While Kath was laying a foundation for compassionate ministry by building up trust through her part-time work on the estate, Barrie was gaining valuable business experience in the marketing and financial management of large corporate organizations, a commercial understanding of sales development and legal and property matters, a knowledge of how to present official proposals and funding applications and some expertise in handling personnel issues. Each of these skills has subsequently proved to be providential.

* * * * *

Probably most helpful to me were the principles I learned in relation to staff management. The Stobart Group had a very open strategy and encouraged people to develop. The first thing we were taught was: "Find your replacement, because you can't move up the ladder unless there is someone to replace you!" As you grow older, there is a next stage to this. You have to find your replacement, so that they can learn from you and surpass you! Then, when you are no longer there, the work will still continue.

Other slogans that were often heard at Stobarts are: 'You'll get over the price, but you'll never get over a bad job' (meaning: It's better to pay more than have to settle for something obviously inferior, which will never get better) and 'First loss is best loss' (meaning: When something isn't working, stop it. Don't be afraid of change). I also learned to 'sail close to the line'. If I don't stay close to the absolute limit of what is legal and possible, I leave a gap for the competition to fill. This is something that many Christians feel uncomfortable with. They like to be cautious and leave a wide margin. But when I leave a margin I am ceding ground and missing out on kingdom gains. We sometimes miss out on opportunities.

I have an aggressive approach to targeting needs. When you target needs, you establish relationships, and when you have relationships you are living the gospel! I don't mind what it takes, but I want to establish relationships. When we have access to people we can meet their needs holistically. Then I can speak to them about church: 'You trusted us in that. Can't you now trust us in this too?' They know I'm not just there to proselytize, to pick on vulnerable people. When I'm meeting needs unconditionally, I'm living the gospel. It's important for me to use all the means and resources available to me to address the needs in this community. I don't want to turn away anyone in need. I want to be absolutely available to them!

One thing that is often difficult to negotiate in Christian work is what to do when team members have different opinions about what the next step should be. When God put Kath and me together, he would speak to us individually about the same thing. It often happened that I would sit down and Kath would say, 'I know what you're thinking.' So, there was always a unity between us—and we have held on to that, even when other people joined the team. Unless there is consensus about a new direction, we don't take it. We have to move in unison if we are following God in this work. That's the way forward.

It seems as if God took a long time to prepare me for my work on the estate, but it does require mature decision-making skills. If I had come here as a 25-year-old, the work would already have collapsed. For example, 18 months ago we were suddenly inundated with different opportunities for development all at the same time. My business instinct is to go for every one—I feel I shouldn't miss any. But as a team we recognized that there was a danger that we could go where God wasn't leading and could get swamped by all the demands. So, we remembered what our primary vision was and as soon as we focused on that, opportunities arose that fell within that original vision. We are following God. We're not looking for glory for ourselves.

18

Back to School

One of the most significant opportunities that next arose in the work of the Trust came about in conjunction with Morton School. This is the closest secondary school to Raffles Estate and the one that most of the local youth attend. For many months the Trust had been looking for a chance to talk to the headteacher about the possibility of our youthworkers getting involved in assemblies or in the classrooms, particularly because their work on the estate had already given them a relationship with many of the youngsters at risk. But the doors stayed firmly shut.

Then suddenly Barrie had an invitation from the headteacher, requesting help from the Trust with pupils who were in danger of exclusion. The invitation came because there was a possibility that significant funding might be available to the school for such a project, which had to be set up in conjunction with a local community body. The Trust jumped at the opportunity, and even undertook to set it up whether or not the school got the funding!

Soon a pastoral care programme was put in place at the school, funded by Tearfund in conjunction with the Cumbria Community Foundation. It offered teachers the opportunity to refer pupils with emotional or relational difficulties to someone who was skilled in listening to them one-to-one and who could help them to work through the things that troubled them. These issues have included coming to terms with being bereaved or being adopted and relationship problems with parents or their partners among many other things.

'Sometimes they have no one they trust who they can talk to. Often they need the freedom just to cry about something hurtful in their lives which they are powerless to change,' Ruth explains. It helps enormously if the youthworker or counsellor already has an understanding of the young person's particular social and family situations—something the Trust workers often do have as a result of contact in the youth clubs on Raffles or on the bus, but something that teachers in school no longer have the time or opportunity to acquire.

It's also typical with children at risk that anything—even very insignificant or ordinary things—can serve as a trigger for them to 'kick off'. For example, when a teacher shouts at them a child's eyes may cloud over and they may shut down to any further communication. What triggers them is related to whatever abuse they have come to associate with it, and once it happens, their survival instinct will make them do anything to get excluded. It's their way of saying, 'I want to get out of here.' Understanding this and handling such situations takes special skills that the average schoolteacher is not trained in—but the Trust's youthworkers are.

In addition to the pastoral care programme, other opportunities arose at Morton—such as the chance to develop an after-school programme aimed at extending the skills of early school-leavers. The Government has been providing increasing support for greater community involvement with schools, and it was sponsoring this programme, called Third Session. Morton invited the Living Well Trust to become a partner in this venture and as a result after-school clubs were set up in the Family Centre on Raffles for pupils who wouldn't go to anything provided in the school but were happy to go to the centre. The modules that focused on building self-esteem through arts-and-crafts activities and flower-arranging were well attended.

As a direct result of the Trust's help on this front, Morton was one of only 37 schools across the UK to attain 'established' status through the Government's 'Quality in Study Support' programme. The

Trust has since achieved 'emerging' status in its own right under QiSS, and is the only voluntary body in the county to have done so.

At the same time, Barrie, Kath and Ruth had noticed that on the streets around the Family Centre there was always an appreciable number of young people wandering around during school hours. They usually fell into one of two categories: those who were still in mainstream education but were temporarily excluded and those who had become voluntarily disengaged from mainstream education or had been permanently excluded from it.

Ruth approached her steering group for advice on how to develop some provision for these youngsters. It was clear from the comments from the educational professionals that there was no 'knot at the end of the rope', which meant simply that once a young person had disengaged from mainstream education they simply dropped off the end of the rope. So, the Trust decided to become a knot for those young people with whom they had already built up a relationship.

Concentrating on pupils from the west of Carlisle, the Trust developed a project in collaboration with the attendance and inclusion unit of the Education Welfare Service and their pupil referral unit and with support from the headteacher of Morton School. A qualified teacher was appointed to take charge of the academic provision. At the time of going to press, the project has been running for 12 months, delivering full-time education in the community, to eight pupils in the Family Centre and 10 at Morton. All are registered on Asdan education projects, and every one will receive at least one accredited qualification for their efforts. (The Asdan Gold award is now considered equivalent to a GCSE grade B.) In December 2004, one silver and four bronze Asdan awards were given to pupils on the project who, to quote Morton's deputy head, would have been 'permanently excluded without the work of the Trust'.

This is intensive and difficult work. It takes considerable effort to establish and maintain the sound relationships necessary for these young people to build their future. Funding for this work is not easy to obtain, and some pupils have been taught without external funding, because the Trust is committed not to turn any child away from education (often these young people have already experienced multiple traumatic rejections in their short lives). It is an essential part of the Living Well Trust's witness in the community that no person in need is to be rejected or turned away. If one side of an educational project fails to engage a young person, we simply adopt a different tack and try a new method or a new topic to catch their imagination.

For those still at school but in danger of exclusion, the Trust has expanded its involvement at Morton. In January 2004 a problem arose with a group of Year 9 pupils who were causing serious disruption in the school. The headteacher asked the Trust to help in providing them with some structured physical health and social education skills. Funding was eventually obtained from the local Kingmoor Park Charitable Trust and the Tudor Trust.

For three afternoons a week the pupils attended sessions run at the Family Centre on the estate. Half their time in the centre was spent doing National Curriculum work and the other half was spent developing a new alternative curriculum which focused on personal development through topics like relationships, boundaries and self-esteem.

It became apparent that in order to allow the Family Centre to develop its own youthwork curriculum it would be better to separate it from the programme for Morton School and for the latter to be run on the school premises. Fortunately there was space available and an unused wing of the school was handed over to the Trust for refurbishment. It has since become known as 'the Den' (an acronym for 'developing, empowering, nurturing').

The Den is flexible in meeting the needs of the pupils. The most crucial thing it is host to is a reintegration programme that provides education in a different kind of setting for pupils in danger of exclusion. At the same time, it's a space where school-based youthworkers can take special sessions with a whole year group or with particular individuals in need of emotional and social support. During its first year, more than a hundred pupils took part in educational activities in the Den each week, and from January 2005 10 pupils will receive full educational provision there. This partnership between the Trust and the school is proving to be a winner, and Ruth has already been approached by two other local secondary schools to set up something similar for pupils in danger of disengaging from education or being excluded.

Neither has the success of the Den been lost on the pupils themselves, who are proud of the fact that they are part of this pioneering 'experiment'. When Ruth excitedly told a few lads recently that she had been approached by another headteacher in Carlisle who is interested in setting up something similar in his school, the response was immediate: 'Ah, that's just copying! Remember to put in the contract that we were the first! We have the copyright!'

19

A Worshipping Community

Barrie is not ashamed to confess that from the beginning it was the idea of a worshipping community on Raffles Estate that inspired him most: 'I firmly believe that we have to bring Christ to people—the Holy Spirit will bring people to Christ.'

* * * * *

In order to provide the people on the estate with an opportunity to worship in their own community, we developed a series of services together with the local Anglican church, St Barnabas'. These 'Songs of Praise' services were held in the Community Hall on a Sunday afternoon so as not to clash with any other church services. First they were held quarterly and then they became more frequent until in the end they were monthly. They were designed around the cultural and spiritual needs of the local community and bore little resemblance to their namesake on TV! As a result, they were well attended by people who wouldn't normally have considered coming into a church.

By normal standards, the services were totally chaotic. As we were dealing with unchurched (or dechurched) people, the pace was fast and furious, with nothing lasting more than five minutes. Games, drama, puppets, quizzes, modern choruses, all played a role in bringing the people to a point of worship. These were fun times and so off-the-wall that they were exciting to take part in, although pretty frightening too.

It was frightening for me because my normal preaching style was to stand woodenly behind the pulpit and speak from notes. But here I had to develop a street-preaching style, with no pulpit, moving among the people, with no notes because eye contact was essential at all times. And the people needed attention-grabbing content.

When the services started, I would get about three to five minutes to speak, during which I had to get used to whatever distractions came my way. Young children rode their tricycles up and down the hall, smiling sweetly as they passed me, while some adults decided that the service was like a Working Men's Club event and as soon as the 'turn' came on—ie my 'sermon'—they started chatting to a neighbour, and not quietly either. Regular toilet exits ensured a constant flow of people moving around. Songs had to be rhythmical and choruses were much in demand, as were old favourites. Even so, I can remember one carol service when we had 'Silent Night' and only the handful of Christians present sang, while everyone else was deep in conversation.

In church-planting terms, this was not the accepted, traditional model. Within the Church of the Nazarene in the UK it is more typical for a small fellowship to start meeting and then, as it grows, look for a suitable venue. Once established in its own building, it will then begin to organize outreach events and run various activities on its premises, which could include compassionate ministry. In the case of Raffles, things happened exactly the other way round. The Living Well Trust was set up to provide compassionate ministry to the needy people of the estate, and the church followed as a natural consequence of the work already done over several years. Moreover it was planted at the instigation of the local people.

Nevertheless the initiative worked and God blessed it. People became used to the concept of worship, they learned a new respect for church and they found a new desire to learn more about God and have a relationship with him. The new Christians on the estate thrived in the atmosphere of these services. They felt comfortable at them and at ease, and found them relevant—and wanted weekly services like these to be held on the estate.

At this point it became clear to Kath and me that the normal way of organizing and running a church in the Nazarene denomination would also not be appropriate for Raffles. A new approach was needed for this culture and situation. For example, they decided not to have any formal membership. Those who meet on a Sunday are the church. The reason for this is that many people on the estate are so reluctant to commit themselves to anything that they would rather not go to church if they felt under any obligation to 'join' it.

It also seemed wrong to me to preach a strong message of unconditional love to these people while insisting on the condition of membership. So, instead, the 'members' of this church are simply those who are regular and faithful in attendance and who express Jesus in their lives. They are not discouraged from becoming formal members, and many have chosen to do so, but it isn't a prerequisite for those who want to serve in the church or vote at church meetings—though everyone accepts that the leaders of the church, its elders and deacons, have to be members, and no one has any qualms about this.

In the end we decided to take a step of faith and start a weekly service on a Sunday evening as soon as the Family Centre was opened. We would try it for six months, and if 10 people from the estate were coming every week we would continue it after that. And so my dream of a worshipping community became a reality: as the weeks went by, people became more relaxed in worship, more reflective and ready and hungry to learn. At first I could speak for only five minutes, then eight, then 10, and now it's possible to speak for 20 or 25 minutes without interruption. We suddenly realized recently that the once rapid-fire services we used to hold, which majored on activity and variety, have now changed. People are content to worship and experience the presence of God. Games, quizzes and dramas are still part of the service, but they are far less important than they used to be.

It was always a challenge for me, when speaking at the services, to find the point of engagement, the cultural relevance of a passage. It's essential in this sort of culture to ensure that people can easily understand how the Bible applies to their own situation and what it means for them. My once-loved word studies and theological interpretations and so on had to be thrown out of the window, to make way for a new approach. It has meant that the Bible has become alive and fresh for me too in a new way.

The Sunday service was moved to the morning by popular request. It lasts for an hour and is followed every week by another hour devoted to a meal. The fact that we are prepared to spend time eating together sends a powerful message of acceptance in this community. Once a month the church provides a free roast dinner for everyone who comes to the service, and on the other three or four Sundays we serve sandwiches and cakes.

By being established as a church on the estate we have been able to take advantage of the rites-of-passage services—baptisms, marriages and funerals. These are significant opportunities to come alongside people who wouldn't normally engage with church but for whom these occasions are still important. The chance to make Jesus relevant at these times is not to be missed, and sharing in the joy of christenings and weddings allows us to get close to the families concerned. But what has truly surprised us is the way in which God has used funerals. They are times when the whole estate (which functions very much as a community) mourns. People are vulnerable and barriers come down. In grieving with the families at such times, we prove the relevance of the love of God.

In addition to the Sunday services and the services that mark the rites of passage, we also started weekly Bible studies. These became very special times of teaching. Here, too, food plays an important part, as we meet over a meal at 6.30pm before we move into the time of study. We were amazed to find that more non-Christians attended the Bible studies than Christians. What an opportunity!

We tried a number of study resources, such as the Alpha course and Christianity Explored, but invariably they required a kind of conceptual thinking that didn't come naturally to these people. It became clear to me that the only way forward was to write my own material, aimed at these people's level. We began with a series around the theme of 'What the Bible says about how to cope with…' We explored topics such as forgiveness, holding grudges, temptation, guilt and fear. More recently we looked at the life, times and ministry of Paul, his journeys and his sufferings—all of which we tried to apply to our situations today.

It was surprising to many that for over two years we didn't once open a Bible in these meetings. Such was the level of trust people had in us, it was sufficient for me when applying biblical principles to say, 'My Bible says…' But it was an advantage not to open a Bible in the studies. It meant that people didn't feel nervous about coming if they had a problem with literacy or didn't know the difference between the Old and New Testaments or the order of the books of the Bible. It was far more important to establish biblical truths and principles than to memorize Bible verses.

After the meal, I speak on the topic for discussion and then the meeting breaks up into groups which discuss the questions I've set, often at length. Sometimes if the discussion veers off into a particular issue important to someone, we follow wherever it leads so that no one goes home with any unanswered questions. The studies have become amazing times of blessing both for the new Christians and for those who lead the groups. It's exciting to hear people express their faith in a way that is relevant to their understanding. People have come to the Lord when they realized that the simple truth of the gospel related to them in their own situations.

One night I spoke on forgiveness. A new woman attended that evening who at the time could only be described as a very wicked person. Other residents lived in fear of her. If anyone crossed her or her family, they had to leave the estate. She had abused her own body and as a result had suffered two strokes and had lost a leg. She was bitter to the core because she had lost her son in a car crash—and because his friend not only survived it but went on to marry her son's girlfriend, who was pregnant with her son's child.

As we spoke about forgiveness, a real sense of God's Spirit came over the meeting. The woman was broken, as she understood for the first time that she could be forgiven, and realized too that she was free to forgive! Later, in her own home, she asked Jesus to forgive her and become her Lord. Her life was transformed and she has now become a potent witness for the gospel of Jesus Christ.

Another woman described the effect of Jesus in her life as being 'like a coat of varnish: he sealed me in, and now I'm no longer vulnerable to whatever others say or do.' Testimonies like these encourage the team as they see God active in a powerful and relevant way in the lives of people who have never experienced him before.

There is no doubt that God is on the move on Raffles Estate. In the Community Church, as people are learning to pray for one another they see how God answers their prayers, not just about the big issues but also about the little things they may have assumed he would not be interested in. It's interesting that the city-centre property that the Trust recently acquired is about 25 yards from where the first Church of the Nazarene was located in Carlisle back in the 1930s, before it moved to the Belle Vue area of the city. It's as if the church has come back home!

And it's not just the people from the estate who are blessed but the workers of the Living Well Trust as well, most of whom attend the morning service at the Community Church. Ruth, for example, is a deacon and worship leader, and she has discovered that she has a real ability to teach other churches about working with and understanding disengaged young people.

The members of the Community Church are also learning about the gifts of the Spirit. They find that God has provided his Body with gifts of healing, discernment, teaching, administration and so on. No one is threatened by these gifts as they are all used in an orderly and biblical way for the benefit of everyone. Certainly I'm not threatened when anyone has gifts I haven't received. On the contrary, I rejoice in it and challenge them to develop these gifts.

As far as visions go, we never say of any suggestion that it's 'impossible'. We have no preconceived ideas of what should be happening. We do take things as they come and don't rule anything out. We are not under law. If we get a suggestion, we say: 'Let's test it!' If it's of God, it'll happen! Nothing is 'normal' here—or maybe this is normal. We should never box in the Spirit. I want to be next to the person with the vision, because that's where all the excitement is.

Afterword

The Living Well Trust team regularly take time to remind ourselves of our original vision, to focus and to remember the lessons we have learned. As we look back it is hard to believe what God has been doing on Raffles. As far as the Trust is concerned, in its first year our turnover was £23,000 and just six years later, in the year to December 2004, it exceeded £300,000! But this is only one way to measure how our work has grown.

Every aspect of the work is facing exciting developments. As part of the Carlisle West Children's Centre, the Family Centre now plays an important role in the provision of family support and health services. The opening of a city-centre facility for the support of victims of domestic violence and drug and alcohol abuse is also a milestone. The increasing demand for school-based educational support, as well as the development of our own alternative curriculum for those who have missed all opportunities for education, demonstrates a growing acceptance of the professionalism the Trust now offers.

The Bus, and the possibility of a second such bus to try to meet the rising demand for its services, illustrates that Christians can successfully reach out to what are seen as a hard-to-engage sector of society. The Community Church (which has just employed a youth pastor to develop culturally appropriate and relevant programmes for young people in contact with the church and the Trust) ensures that attention is focused on spiritual matters.

As for you who have read this story, I hope you will find the following guidelines useful in your own life and ministry:

1. God can use anybody in a wonderful way. One thing the workers at Living Well are all convinced of is that they are very ordinary people! But they also know that when God calls people, he takes into account the whole package of their life experience and gifts—

and in that respect the Living Well team is hand-picked with a unique combination of skills and abilities matched to the needs of the work.

2. You too are very personally loved, accepted and needed by God. Unless you understand this, so that it gets into your marrow, you will not be able to convey this essential message to anyone else. You need to experience it for yourself!

3. This book shares some of the theological principles, the truths that one has to understand when one sets out to work in compassionate outreach. Many of these lessons were learned in practice, and you too will have to learn them in the same way. But it helps to be warned!

4. Through all the stories in this book we have simply shared how God has worked in our case. Maybe you will find positive lessons in our experience, maybe you will find cautions of what to avoid, but we hope it will help you to persevere. In particular, remember that apparently dead periods have proved with hindsight to have been fertile times of learning and training for the workers and of essential preparation for the community. Without them the whole work would have collapsed under the pressure that was caused by the subsequent growth!

5. In this book we celebrate the diversity of God's church, his Body. Not everyone received the vision, and some were called to support the work only from a distance while others were challenged to make huge changes in their lifestyle. Some 'only' pray for it, or 'only' give money towards it, or 'only' help with menial tasks around the place. But no one member of the team can be the saviour or the head. Jesus is the only Saviour, and he is the Head.

Barrie Thomas
2005

Appendix 1

Stories that Illustrate Some Practical Lessons Learned

1. The change God makes in a person's life is real and significant but not instant!

Vivian has grown up on Raffles. She had a traumatic childhood and was twice raped as a teenager, and from there slid into a series of abusive relationships that spiralled out of control into drug and alcohol abuse. Her four young children were taken from her into care, and when her boyfriend at the time overdosed on heroin she finally cracked up and was committed to a psychiatric unit.

Seven months later she was released late one evening, with nowhere to go because her council house had been taken while she was in hospital. She had no money, no belongings, just a piece of paper in her hand with the prescription for her medication.

A family from the Community Church who had known her for a long time offered her accommodation until another council house became available. She was much better, but continued to suffer from the consequences of her past life. To this day she finds it hard to be completely free from the bondage of substance addiction.

However, she has experienced God's touch and can now pray for her children. She has also discovered that she can write poetry and this has become a vehicle for expressing what God has done for her. The Living Well workers regularly pray for and with Vivian. She is a gifted woman who could be useful to God on the estate. We believe that one day she will be able to give all praise to him for her total release into life! But God has time—as much time as it takes for real and significant healing to happen in her life.

Vivian has come a long way already since the day the community policeman asked the Trust for help. She had failed to pay some fines and had been issued with a court order. The police van came to take her to the court but she simply refused to get into it. It reminded her of the day she had been taken into psychiatric care. Kath and Graham spoke to her and the police agreed that they could take her to court. This was only the first miracle of the day!

Normally Vivian would be kept in a cell at the police station until it was time for her case to be heard, but again she was terrified by the prospect of being confined, as it reminded her of her confinement in the psychiatric hospital. Kath and Graham prayed quietly with her and a second miracle happened: she was allowed to stay in the public reception area!

As she owed a lot of money and had no means of earning it, it seemed certain that the only outcome of her hearing would be a prison sentence. Kath thought about this and while they were waiting she told Vivian the story of how God had intervened and released Peter from prison in a miraculous way. Kath was bold in her belief that God could do the same for her.

The atmosphere in the courtroom was tense as the magistrates listened to her case. Kath could confirm that the Trust had been active in supporting her. She could also explain the difficult circumstances Vivian had already come through. Finally the verdict was given: provided she could pay the court costs of £45 within the next 48 hours, all the fines would be quashed and she could be released immediately. Vivian knew that God had intervened in her life in a special way. He had indeed set her free!

Although she continues to struggle with her dependence on medication to block out the memories of the past, Vivian also has a smile that on one of her good days can light up a room. We long to see the amazing transformation God has started in her life complete!

2. *God works in mysterious ways.*

Mary and her two daughters, Sally and Jo, are only young Christians, and so when difficulties come they tend to resort to the tactics they used to use in the old days. This tests the faith of those who live alongside them, and it tests whether our commitment to them is real or just academic, whether it is something we act out in the nitty-gritty of daily living or just something we talk about in sermons.

So, when Sally had a particularly upsetting experience recently and instinctively lashed out with her old weapons against Jo and Mary, we were not surprised. But we also knew that we had to tackle the situation because of the effect it could have on others in the church, and so we arranged a meeting to encourage reconciliation.

Unfortunately there was no reconciliation, because Sally felt so deeply hurt that although Jo and Mary asked her to forgive them, she couldn't do it. Still, God is at work and what seemed to be a failure has had surprising results. Sally had brought a non-Christian friend along with her to the meeting, and this woman was amazed to see how Christians acted. She heard the talk of forgiveness and she saw the love Jo and Mary showed and their willingness to forgive. This witnessed to her far more effectively than any sermon could have done.

This woman's sense of the reality of God was further heightened when her father died the next day. Was God preparing her for a special encounter with him? Others too who have heard of that meeting have felt deeply spoken to and have wanted to seek forgiveness from people they have wronged.

God's vision is so much larger than ours. It's amazing what he can do when we recognize our weakness and inability and hand the situation over to him. All the glory be to him!

3. If we can't show the love of Christ at Christmas, when can we?

Now that we are established as a church on the estate we can make the most of special celebrations—and celebrating Christmas offers a great opportunity. It's a feature of the work, though, that things don't always go as planned! For example, at our first Christmas service we invited Santa. The dear man who undertook to play the part arrived full of ho-ho-ho and jollity, unaware of the whispered exchanges between some of the young boys in the room: 'You hold him down and I'll get his beard!'

In the end the poor chap had to be rescued—only to be chased home, still in full costume, by one of the local dogs, who clearly was not pleased to have been overlooked for a present! The next Sunday after the service he said to Kath and Fay that, much as he had enjoyed being Santa, please would they choose someone else next time!

Christmas is particularly exciting for children and in the Community Church we have started a tradition of providing a gift for each child in each family we are in contact with. If we have had contact with one child but know there are four more in the family, all five will receive a present. The Belle Vue Church has joined this initiative and it now holds a special 'gift' service before Christmas for which members of the congregation are asked to buy a gift for a child up to £5 in value. As many as 35 presents are provided in this way, and the Living Well Trust purchases the rest on a similar budget. For Christmas 2004, a total of more than 200 were handed out.

This may seem an expensive initiative, but you can't put a price on the joy these gifts bring. And by collecting goods throughout the year and working through organizations such as Inkind Direct, which handles surplus stock from stores, we maximize the quality and range of toys we can buy for each £5!

Nativity services are also a precious part of the Christmas celebrations. One particular service stands out in our memories. The highlight on this occasion came in the final scene with the arrival of the Wise Men. One of them was played by Jeff, a young boy who suffers from cerebral palsy. Earlier in the year the Community Church had raised over £800 for a specially constructed walking frame for him, and this was to be his big day. The frame was decorated like a camel and Jeff was dressed up in his costume. There wasn't a dry eye in the church as Jack struggled determinedly to walk all the way up the aisle without help. Every step was an effort and by the time he arrived at the front he was exhausted. When he reached baby Jesus and handed him his gift and bowed his head, even the preacher couldn't hold back the tears!

4. If God has a sense of humour, so should we.

One day, the police stopped a vehicle just outside the Family Centre and arrested the driver. Jock was Jeff's father and he was well known to the Trust workers as he and his family regularly attended the Centre. Also, at the age of 30, he had recently been baptized in the Community Church. Unfortunately he had a history of car-related crime and a prison sentence was likely if he got another conviction and so, given his home situation, the ages of his children and the important role he played in the daily care of his son, the Trust agreed to support him in court.

On the day of his hearing, Barrie went to testify on his behalf and explain his circumstances to the magistrates. There didn't seem to be much hope that Jock would get off lightly and when they finally announced a three-month custodial sentence his friends and family felt their hearts sink. But then, to everyone's astonishment, one of the magistrates added that, in the light of Jock's home situation and the support the Trust had offered to give him, his sentence would be suspended as long as he could pay the court fees!

Later that afternoon, when Barrie got back to the Centre, he was greeted with great hilarity. It turned out that a reporter had been present in court and the billboards for the local newspaper now boldly declared: 'Pastor saves Raffles man from prison'. If nothing else, it raised the profile of the Trust on the estate. It was also a powerful witness to God's power in action, to save people in their particular needs.

5. Allow others to experience God in their own way, and never try to prescribe what he may do!

From time to time Carol joined in the activities at the Family Centre—the women's lunches, the Christmas events. She really enjoyed these occasions and it was good to see her smiling because it meant she had managed to forget her cares for a moment. She was in her early forties and she carried many burdens. Her son was in prison and her daughter was a drug addict, not fit to look after her own child.

Carol had a nervous manner when she talked. She spoke loudly and rapidly, and the effect was not unlike machine-gun fire. She rarely hung around and never just dropped in for a chat. So, it was strange when she turned up on the doorstep one morning, apparently wanting just that. Time went by and still she lingered. She seemed to feel at home and quite relaxed. Eventually it was time for our regular Bible study and prayer meeting. We wondered whether to cancel it, to save her embarrassment, but in the end we decided to go ahead after all and simply invite her to stay as long as she felt comfortable. To our amazement she stayed the whole time. She seemed calm and at peace, as if the burdens had been lifted from her shoulders.

Two days later Carol died suddenly and unexpectedly at home. Her funeral service was held in the Community Church. She had never been to a church service and we never found out what had happened that day—but we believe that she met God before her death and that we will see her in eternity.

6. Providing food is an essential part of every meeting.

The work of the Trust has developed and changed format over the years, but our commitment to provide love, care and food has remained the same. It has become a well-established principle in all our work that we provide food during our meetings. This is not just a 'nicety'—it addresses real, acute and disabling hunger! For example, at the end of one Loaves and Fishes session the workers noticed that one of the boys was not only putting food onto his plate but also stuffing supplies up his coat sleeves. The sausage rolls were disappearing so fast they decided to have a word with him, to explain that he was free to come back for seconds but it would show good manners to wait until everyone else had had some first.

Imagine how they felt when he told them that the food he had stashed up his sleeves was not for him but for his little sister at home! It was a shock to think what this said about the level of care in his family.

7. *There is no time off in this work—you're always being watched!*

Today the workers of the Living Well Trust are well aware that they are living in full view of the people of the estate, people who are well trained to spot insincerity, who have been let down so many times by people who offer one thing only to deliver something completely different. Working on the estate means that you're held responsible for what you say—and your actions are constantly measured against your words. The test is: Does what you say on a Sunday match what you do on a wet Thursday afternoon?

Valerie is a typical member of the Raffles community. For more than four years she kept her distance but gradually she started coming closer, even getting involved in Trust activities, until today she actually helps out and takes responsibility in small ways. She readily confesses that she watched carefully to see what agenda lay behind our workers' commitment, but could find only love! As a result she has also started coming to church, not regularly but from time to time.

This is a feature of the work on the estate, that such small commitments are major developments. The people who live on Raffles need time and space to become involved at the pace they can cope with. When someone turns up again after a long absence we don't make a big fuss over them but just welcome them in the same warm way we welcome everyone else.

8. *It's important to look beyond the 'manageable' crises to the deeper things that disable people's lives.*

We have learned over the years of dealing with people on the estate that crisis is a major part of their lives. This used to puzzle us, for with so many crises already present in their lives they seemed to attract new ones at a phenomenal rate. What often appeared to us, when we investigated it, to be a minor issue was regularly whipped up into the subject of frenzied activity as everyone seemed to get involved in the development of the plot. And then, by the next day, all was quickly forgotten! Most of us try to avoid crisis situations in our lives, but on Raffles people were actively seeking them out.

Then we began to understand that in most of the circumstances of their lives the crises people face are so deep and complex and their experiences so painful that they would rather not deal with them. And so instead they look for what we describe as 'a manageable crisis for the day', which bears all the hallmarks of a serious crisis but can be solved inside a day. This makes the people involved feel they have achieved something worthwhile that day—when in truth their biggest achievement has been to distract themselves from the deeper crises that are still unsolved. Unfortunately, with each new day comes, as if by a miracle, a new manageable crisis, and so the cycle goes on.

9. *It isn't our job to persuade people to manage their lives in a way that makes sense to us.*

Closely related to the 'manageable crisis' way of life is the attitude, often expressed on the estate, that the most important thing on any given day is 'to survive the day'. This is applied particularly to the management of personal finances, as when you have few expectations in life you also have little incentive to start planning it. Instead you tend to think only of the present moment, or at most the next 24 hours. Tomorrow seems a million miles away, and planning ahead is a completely unknown concept. Sometimes people have a full purse one day and not a penny the next. It's as if they always expect a miracle to fill the purse up again! So, they often spend their money unwisely on futile things while their food cupboards are empty.

The Trust's workers have a very different culture and so it's hard for us to understand this way of living. It's also difficult to present people who live only for today with the gospel promise of an eternal life to come. That is our challenge!

10. Children are powerful evangelists in their own homes.

Songs and choruses with lively tunes have always been a very important part of all the worship activities related to the Trust and the Community Church. The children especially are quick to pick up the tunes and the words.

Sally attended many of the Trust's youth activities, and she liked the songs she learnt there so much that she asked for a CD-Rom of them all. We later found out that she played the music at home non-stop and even made her father sing along with her! He wouldn't easily be persuaded to attend a worship service, not even a carol service, and yet there he was at home happily singing the words of Christian choruses. Who knows what influence they may have on his life once he starts to understand what they mean?

11. Be flexible when setting rules!

We used to take the children every summer to a small town called
Allonby on the west coast of Cumbria. For some it was their only
chance ever to get to the seaside! At this point we hadn't yet realized
the advantage of making all our trips into 'family' days, which would
leave the responsibility of supervision to the children's own parents.
So, our workers had the nerve-racking task of supervising two
coachloads of children by the sea.

As we arrived at Allonby we always gave the same talk about
safety and explained how they should stow their clothes, shoes and
towels in the bags we provided, so they could be sure to have dry
things to change into after they'd been in the water. And yet year after
year we felt like King Canute trying to stem the tide as we watched the
young lads rushing headlong into the sea without taking a single item
of clothing off first! They ended up wet for the whole day, and were
usually still damp when we boarded the coach for the return journey.

Why did we get so worked up about it? For some children it was
the most exciting day of their lives, and we just needed a good rest
afterwards.

12. Don't make assumptions about what is normal in someone else's home!

One young girl, Denise, used to puzzle us. She always fell asleep as
soon as she arrived at any of the children's clubs, and apparently the
same thing happened daily at school!

We were astonished when we discovered the reason. Apparently
she has such a large family that at her home not just bed space but
even floor space is at a premium. Denise is the youngest and the
smallest and so she had learned to wait until everyone else had settled
down for the night before she could find a small space where she

could curl up and go to sleep. Given the spread of ages in her family it could be quite late before she was able to go to sleep. Her tiredness was the result of years of sleep deprivation. It sounded like a story from a previous century!

13. *Learn not to show panic when things go wrong!*

There have been many potentially dangerous moments on the two buses. The community police may record 'all quiet on the Western Front' on nights when The Bus is operating, but that doesn't mean that everything always runs smoothly on it!

Gary once pulled out a powerful air pistol on The Bus. When Graham instinctively grabbed hold of the barrel, Gary threatened to shoot him in the hand. Thankfully, Graham kept a calm exterior and quietly told him what damage he would do to him with his unharmed hand should he try to put that threat into practice Fortunately Gary decided not to call his bluff, but it was a scary moment.

14. *The more easily you are exasperated or embarrassed, the more often you will be.*

When we first began Loaves and Fishes, some of the older women from the Belle Vue Church offered to help. But this wasn't 'children's work' as they had known it!

One woman, Miss Thompson, was finally driven to the limits of her patience one Saturday when Kath and Fay decided to introduce the youngsters to clay modeling and asked them to make models of biblical figures. It took no time at all before some of the boys decided to start making men whose sensitive body parts were rather larger than average. Miss Thompson was clearly upset by this—but as fast as she flattened the offending models the boys remade them. That is, until they tired of that and turned their attention instead to the more profitable making of 'gange' pots ('gange' is the local word for cannabis). Miss Thompson no longer turned up as a helper after that!

Another volunteer, Eileen, had been born with only part of her left arm—not that anyone could tell from her driving, craftwork and general all-round ability. But few things escape the scrutiny of the children on the estate and her arm has fascinated many of the younger children. One day she was trying to explain to a five-year-old that God made us because he loved us. The child's immediate reply was: 'Well, he can't have loved you much because you must have been really bad to have been made like that!' Fortunately Eileen has a good sense of humour and could laugh about it. Secure in God's love for her, she didn't have to feel hurt or embarrassed.

15. Ask God—he cares about every detail!

When the Family Centre was opened, we needed a suitable carpet for the function room. The brand we had in mind was a highly durable carpet, but soft to the touch. We asked the local distributor to give us a quotation. When he came in, he was carrying a sample that so perfectly matched the colour of the paintwork we thought he must have sneaked in beforehand to check. But no, this just happened to be the end-of-line remnant stock he was keen to sell off.

The cost for this type of flooring was about £20 a square metre, but discounts could bring it down to £15 or even £12. However, he offered us the remnant he had brought along for £7.50 a square metre! It was still too expensive for us, though, and we offered £5 a square metre. In the end we settled on a price of £5.50.

Needless to say, we don't view this as a coincidence. God knows exactly what we need and takes care of every detail, including in the practical things of life.

16. Never forget you're taking part in a supernatural battle!

The year 2002 ended on a particularly sad note, though there was also a note of rejoicing at God's work in people's lives. A young man, Chris, had died at the end of November after a five-year battle against cancer. He was one of the bravest people we have met and handled the pain and confusion of dying so young with great courage. He had known Kath since he was a little boy at school, and always held her in high esteem.

He was a positive young man, but as the end came closer he became frightened of going to sleep in case he never woke up again. He had great concerns over his coming death: it seemed so unfair to him that he should die in the prime of life while others seem to live long past the age when they can be useful to society. We tried to answer his questions honestly, and where we didn't have any answer we simply shared our own bewilderment.

We tried to tell Chris about the path to eternal life. He had very little understanding of Christianity, and we just told him to reach out to Jesus and pray to him. One day he asked us to see him to sort out some concerns he had over his funeral arrangements, and rather shyly he told us that he had tried to pray, and would continue to do so. It was the last time we saw him alive.

I felt so inadequate and I shared my feelings with a friend, who greatly encouraged me by reminding me of the power of the Holy Spirit to intervene and clear the way for a person to come to faith. In his email to me he wrote in large letters: 'BUT YOU DID NOT SEE HIM FOR NO REASON.' Even though we didn't see any evidence of the work of the Holy Spirit, it doesn't mean that he wasn't present and working in Chris. I do not know what reconciliation, if any, took place between Chris and God. I could not affirm to his family that he had certainly come to faith, but neither could I deny it.

The funeral was an extremely sad affair, as was to be expected, but it gave the Living Well team a powerful opportunity to share the love of Jesus with a family that normally would not have turned to the church for help. Even in the pain of grief we have a message of love and hope to offer and we can demonstrate that even at their weakest every person can be loved, accepted and needed.

After every funeral we have taken on the estate we have felt more accepted and new opportunities have opened up in families as people came to respect our commitment to serving them.

17. People respond imaginatively when a new truth makes sense to them.

At one Sunday service Barrie was explaining that we all need to find release from the heavy baggage we carry about with us and the only place we can do this is at the foot of the cross. He illustrated this by saying that if you stood at the foot of the cross you would find there bags with his name on them, and went on to speak of others who had left their baggage there.

During the refreshments after the service he was surprised when a young woman came and told him that the bags she had left at the door of the Centre were no longer there. Barrie immediately called for a telephone so that he could report the theft to the police, but of course he had got completely the wrong impression. Other team members had to calm him down before he could understand what this young woman was trying to say. She had understood that she had been carrying baggage from her past. To her, the Centre was as sacred a place as anywhere and she now felt she had left those issues at the door, so that when she left the Centre she sensed a new freedom, just as he had explained in the service. She hadn't lost anything she wanted to keep, but was praising God for her release.

As long as she can continue to leave her bags at the front door, they will be removed and she won't have to carry them any more.

Appendix 2

A Biblical and Theological Basis

The challenge for any Christian ministry is to ensure that it has a sound biblical understanding of its reason for existence, an understanding that can be relied on to defend or evaluate the work at any given moment. Such an understanding must be robust enough to correspond to living reality and it must incorporate the life experience gained.

Broadly speaking, the Living Well Trust finds its biblical mandate in what is known as the Great Commission of Jesus to his disciples, as recorded in Matthew 28:18–20 and Mark 16:15–16. Recently the church has understood this command to be addressed to all believers in all ages, but has it always acted in line with God's mission when it comes to the methods it has employed to fulfil this Great Commission? It hasn't always been careful to put it into practice in the spirit of the words of Jesus recorded in John 20:21: 'As the Father has sent me, I am sending you.'

The key verses that shed light on what Jesus meant by 'As the Father has sent me' are those that explain his understanding of his own liberating mission in Luke 4:18–19. Here he claims to be the one who has been prophetically anointed 'to preach good news to the poor … to proclaim freedom for the prisoners and recovery of sight for the blind, to release the oppressed, to proclaim the year of the Lord's favour'.

With this radical mission statement Jesus clearly challenged those who relied on the Old Testament law for deliverance. Whereas that law condemns them, the gospel is good news for those who are poor, disenfranchised, disengaged, disenchanted, disaffected. Jesus fulfilled the Law and makes mission holistic. Healing, deliverance, justice and concern for the environment all become significant aspects of preaching the good news, aspects from which it cannot be isolated.

Jesus' message of salvation and liberation was deeply rooted in the Levitical idea of Jubilee. It has been said that 'Jesus presupposed that we don't have power, we are power. The gospel unleashes in us processes that can't be stopped—short of social transformation.' Some people resist this. As Ken Gnanakan points out (*Kingdom Concerns*, p25), they hold that 'the role of the church in the realization of such ends as justice, freedom and peace were not spelled out' in the Bible, that it is unclear what, if anything, has been commanded in terms of social transformation. And others, he states (p57), are 'so concentrated on soul winning that practical implications of the gospel are shunned as being liberal theology'.

Going back to the Great Commission, we can now interpret it in the light of Jesus' simple words to the lawyer in Luke 10, where he affirms the Old Testament summary of the Law as 'Love your neighbour as yourself.' This is the least that Jesus expects.

The theology of a holistic ministry of compassion

For the Living Well Trust, the theology for a holistic ministry of compassion rests on three biblical pillars: the mission of God, the incarnation of Christ and the nature of the Kingdom of God.

Mission of God. Surely it is the mission of the Church to discover and then submit to the mission of God, which is defined by Ken Gnanakan (*Kingdom Concerns*, p136) as a mission that 'must seek to rediscover from the pages of the Bible the universality of mission, the width of God's concern for a lost world and the inescapable responsibility laid on every committed Christian to be involved in God's mission'.

But in developing an understanding of the mission of the Church, tension has arisen between those for whom the spoken word is the only true form of evangelism and those who believe that 'without meeting the absolute needs of life, talk about the love of God sounds hollow' (Bruce Nicholls, *Sharing the Good News with the Poor*, p75) and who therefore propose a programme of social action aimed at transformation. As a result, evangelism and social involvement have often been pitted against each other rather than being incorporated as two aspects of one dynamic reality. It has divided the church into two groups: one that focuses on the gospel being preached to sinners (for all have sinned) and one that concentrates on feeding the poor and banishing injustice and hunger rather than on delivering the message of the forgiveness of sins.

It is clear that neither approach on its own can claim to be the mission of God. Evangelism without social action denies the physical relevance of the Kingdom in the here and now and chooses to focus exclusively on the spiritual and the eschatological. But social action without evangelism embraces 'humanization' rather than Christianization and fails to recognize the eschatological aspects of God's kingdom by focusing only on the here and now.

Incarnation. Through the incarnation of Christ, the future rule of God has become a present reality, 'seen and touched' in the words, deeds and person of the man Jesus and those of his followers subsequently. As the Word became flesh, Jesus incarnated all that God is in a living, present, physical person. Just as Jesus lived amongst people and identified with us, so the true Church of Christ must live in love, harmony and freedom within the communities where it finds itself and must identify with them. Understanding Christ's incarnation is the key to becoming relevant to society, for the Incarnation draws the Church out to rely on God rather than become self-reliant (and self-satisfied). Incarnation suggests humiliation, hardship, suffering and rejection, experiences that can be borne only through the power of the Holy Spirit.

Incarnation as a theological concept helps us define the mission of the Church: rather than being trapped into dualistic thinking that separates the realities of the physical and the spiritual, we must move to a new understanding in which evangelism and social action are intertwined to form one cord: we should be 'preaching a message of spiritual salvation while practising a ministry of human well-being' (Bruce Bradshaw, *Bridging the Gap*, piii).

Kingdom of God. God's people must recognize that the Kingdom of God is not just the church but all of creation. The power by which God broke into creation cannot be institutionalized in the church. The Kingdom is greater than either heaven or the church: it includes social justice, righteousness, healing and restoration, and environmental issues. In the context of this full reality, Christians are called to live lives that grow in holiness and love.

In a more holistic approach, the transformation of the physical present is as relevant as spiritual transformation in the future. It is based on the understanding that without transformation there is no Kingdom of God. Transformation is not all that we strive for, but it is certainly an integral part of what we strive for. By ministering to the poor, the sick, the hungry, the prisoners and the oppressed, we declare that the message of the eternal salvation of God is great news for all people—and for all people now. However, if they 'cannot find adequate food, shelter or medical care, a faith that focuses only on their future ultimate purposes is irrelevant' (Bruce Bradshaw, *Bridging the Gap*, p14).

A definition of the 'holistic gospel'

Once we understand the biblical mandate for holistic compassionate ministry based on both the Great Commission and the 'greatest commandment', and the theological mandate built on the three pillars of the mission of God, the incarnation of Christ and the Kingdom of God, it is possible to identify some very practical implications for what we in our denomination describe as 'compassionate ministry'. It has been important to spell these out, for they define what we have in mind, or imagine, when we use the term 'holistic gospel':

- The holistic gospel involves much more than passing a bowl of soup to a homeless person or digging a well to help a whole village get access to a regular supply of clean water, important though these may be. In defining the holistic gospel, we mustn't limit our thinking to the immediate help people need, as it is precisely this that has led to the dualistic thinking in many churches.

- To understand the holistic gospel we must ask risky questions, questions that touch on the politics that shape policy making at local and national levels, questions about society and what lies behind its needs and deprivations. If we treat the symptoms without diagnosing the disease we will only end up supporting the very institutions we are trying to subvertand the very injustices we are trying to end.

- It is important in our understanding of the holistic gospel that education, economics, ecology and medical care are intrinsically valuable aspects of Christ's redemptive work in creation. We need to appreciate that environmental problems, for instance, have theological implications as well as political, economic and cultural ones.

From this we can define the holistic gospel as a true expression of God's shalom, 'the harmony intended by God'. That shalom not only transforms the lives of people and their eternal destiny but also has an impact on their here-and-now environment. It comes to bear on a wide range of life's situations and on nature itself. It is not one event but a process of bringing things into harmony. It isn't limited in time and it can never be completed in time. The holistic gospel exists in the tension between what is ('the already') and what is still to be ('the yet to come').

Compassionate evangelism is the holistic gospel in action. Compassionate ministry has to be a social programme, but not every social programme is a compassionate ministry! And it involves more than just meeting people's needs—it involves love! A compassionate ministry that identifies with people and incarnates the gospel in a culturally relevant way opens up options for the poor. Then the holistic gospel becomes a powerful agent of transformation, here and now as well as for the future.

To summarize: In the context of the holistic gospel, the mission of the church is the mission of God, and the mission of God is linked with a realization of shalom, both in 'the already' and 'the yet to come'. Our eschatology must not be a future-based expectation with no bearing on the present. Rather, we should seek to reconcile the present and the future in a way that demonstrates the immanence of the Kingdom in everyday life through the incarnation of Christ.

If Jesus is our model, then we must embrace his understanding of the Kingdom, which was neither otherworldly or idealistic nor limited to the present. The challenge of the holistic gospel is for the Church to live on what has often been described as 'the kingdom horizon', where past, present and future realities are brought together. When a church recovers its calling to become an advertisement for the Kingdom in this way, its life of witness in the whole community becomes an act of worship, and such worship acts as a witness.

Sources:

Bradshaw, Bruce. *Bridging the Gap: Evangelism, Development and Shalom* (Innovations in Mission Series). Seattle: YWAM Publishing, no date / Monrovia: MARC, 1993.

Gnanakan, Ken. *Kingdom Concerns.* Bangalore: Theological Book Trust / Leicester: IVP, 1990.

Nicholls, Bruce and Beulah Wood. *Sharing the Good News with the Poor.* Carlisle: Paternoster Press / Grand Rapids MI: Baker Book House, 1996.

Contact Info

For the latest news, visit our website at

http://www.livingwelltrust.org.uk

The Living Well Trust is a registered charity in the England & Wales (No. 1080916).

To support the Living Well Trust, or to enquire about volunteer, training or employment opportunities with the Trust, write to
The Living Well Trust
19-23 Shady Grove Road
Carlisle
CA2 7LE
United Kingdom

Book Ordering Info

Compassion & Community: Ordinary People with an Extraordinary Dream
by Illtyd Barrie Thomas

112pp; ISBN 1-903689-32-5
Retail price: £5.99

Order from IVP, freephone 0800 622968
OR contact the publishers at info@piquant.net
OR mail orders to Piquant, PO Box 83, Carlisle, CA3 9GR
(postage for any UK order=£2.95; £(UK) cheques payable to 'Piquant Editions')

Forthcoming in 2006 from Piquant Editions:

Compassionate Community Work: An Introductory Course for Christians,
by Dave Andrews

A practical training course for self-study or group training or to support existing academic modules that are not based on a Christian worldview. With guidelines for students who have completed the course to facilitate other learners.